LATIN AMERICAN POLITICAL, ECONOMIC, AND SECURITY ISSUES

PROGRESS IN PANAMA

POLITICS, ECONOMICS, AND FREE TRADE WITH THE UNITED STATES

LATIN AMERICAN POLITICAL, ECONOMIC, AND SECURITY ISSUES

Additional books in this series can be found on Nova's website under the Series tab.

Additional E-books in this series can be found on Nova's website under the E-book tab.

LATIN AMERICAN POLITICAL, ECONOMIC, AND SECURITY ISSUES

PROGRESS IN PANAMA

POLITICS, ECONOMICS, AND FREE TRADE WITH THE UNITED STATES

CHARLES BOLITNO
EDITOR

NOVINKA

New York

For permission to use material from this book please contact us:
Telephone 631-231-7269; Fax 631-231-8175
Web Site: http://www.novapublishers.com

Additional color graphics may be available in the e-book version of this book.

LIBRARY OF CONGRESS CATALOGING-IN-PUBLICATION DATA

ISBN: 978-1-62417-932-7

Published by Nova Science Publishers, Inc. † New York

CONTENTS

PREFACE

This book examines the close relations between the United States and Panama, stemming in large part from the extensive linkages developed when the Canal was under U.S. control and Panama hosted major U.S. military installations. The current relationship is characterized by extensive counternarcotics cooperation; support to promote Panama's economic, political, and social development; and a bilateral free trade agreement (FTA) that entered into force at the end of October 2012.

Chapter 1 – With five successive elected civilian governments, the Central American nation of Panama has made notable political and economic progress since the 1989 U.S. military intervention that ousted the regime of General Manuel Antonio Noriega from power. Current President Ricardo Martinelli of the center-right Democratic Change (CD) party was elected in May 2009, defeating the ruling center-left Democratic Revolutionary Party (PRD) in a landslide. Martinelli was inaugurated to a five-year term on July 1, 2009. Martinelli's Alliance for Change coalition with the Panameñista Party (PP) also captured a majority of seats in Panama's National Assembly. Panama's service-based economy has been booming in recent years – with a growth rate of 7.6% in 2010 and 10.6% in 2011 – largely because of the ongoing Panama Canal expansion project, now slated for completion in early 2015.

The CD's coalition with the PP fell apart at the end of August 2011when President Martinelli sacked PP leader Juan Carlos Varela as Foreign Minister. Varela, however, retains his position as Vice President. Tensions between the CD and the PP had been growing throughout 2011, largely related to which party would head the coalition's ticket for the 2014 presidential election. Despite the breakup of the coalition, the strength of the CD has grown significantly since 2009 because of defections from the PP and the PRD and it now has a majority on its own in the legislature. President Martinelli's strong approval rating diminished in the aftermath of his break with the PP in 2011, but has recovered recently. President Martinelli's has been criticized by civil society groups and political opponents for taking a heavy-handed approach toward governing and for not being more consultative. At times, strong public protests have resulted in President Martinelli backing away from unpopular policy initiatives. While Panama's next presidential election is not scheduled until May 2014, the country will be gearing up for the race in early 2013. Martinelli is not eligible to run since Panama's Constitution only allows for a president to return to power after two terms (10 years).

Chapter 2 – On June 28, 2007, the United States and Panama signed a free trade agreement (FTA) after two and a half years and 10 rounds of negotiations. Negotiations formally concluded on December 16, 2006, with an understanding that changes to labor, environment, and intellectual property rights chapters would be made pursuant to future congressional input. These changes were agreed to and the FTA was signed in time to be considered under Trade Promotion Authority (TPA) legislation, which expired on July 1, 2007. TPA allows Congress to consider certain trade agreement implementing bills under expedited procedures. Panama's legislature ratified the FTA 58 to 4 on July 11, 2007, but neither the 110th nor the 111th Congress took up the agreement. Eventually, the 112th Congress considered the FTA implementing bill. On July 7, 2011, the House Ways and Means and Senate Finance Committees held simultaneous "mock markups," where they informally approved draft implementing bills. On October 3, 2011, the Obama Administration transmitted final implementing legislation and supporting documents to both houses, as required under TPA. Following committee action, on October 12, 2011, the House agreed to the implementing bill (H.R. 3079) 300-129, followed by the Senate 77-22.

President Obama signed the implementing bill into law on October 21, 2011 (P.L. 112-43, 125 Stat. 427), but the FTA would not enter into force for another year. Panama required that time to complete changes in law necessary to bring it into compliance with the provisions of the FTA. On October 22, 2012, the United States Trade Representative (USTR) exchanged notes with Panama providing for entry into force of the FTA. President Obama implemented the agreement by proclamation on October 29, 2012, and the FTA entered into force on October 31, 2012.

The U.S.-Panama FTA is a comprehensive and reciprocal trade agreement, replacing U.S. unilateral preferential trade treatment extended under the Caribbean Basin Economic Recovery Act (CBERA), the Caribbean Basin Trade Partnership Act (CBTPA), and the Generalized System of

Preferences (GSP). Some 88% of U.S. commercial and industrial exports will become duty-free upon implementation, with remaining tariffs phased out over a 10-year period. Over 50% of U.S. farm exports to Panama also will achieve immediate duty-free status, with tariffs and tariff rate quotas (TRQs) on select farm products to be phased out by year 17 of the agreement (year 20 for rice). The FTA also consummates understandings on telecommunications, services trade, government procurement, investment, and intellectual property rights.

The final text of the U.S.-Panama FTA incorporates changes based on the bipartisan agreement of May 10, 2007, crafted by the Bush Administration and leadership in the 110th Congress. These include adoption of enforceable labor standards, compulsory membership in multilateral environmental agreements, and an easing of restrictions on developing country access to generic drugs, provisions that go beyond those in previous U.S. bilateral FTAs and multilateral trade rules. Concerns raised in Congress on labor and tax transparency issues were also addressed by Panama in statute and by ratification of a Tax Information and Exchange Agreement (TIEA) with the United States. The TIEA provides greater tax transparency in support of curbing illicit financial transactions associated with money laundering activities. This report covers issues related to the U.S.-Panama FTA from the beginning of the negotiations in April 2004 until the FTA entered into force on October 31, 2012.

Chapter 3 – *Area:* 75,517 sq. km. (29,157 sq. mi.); slightly smaller than South Carolina. Panama occupies the southeastern end of the isthmus forming the land bridge between North and South America.

Cities: Capital--Panama City (430,299), Panama District (880,691), Panama Province (1,713,000)). *Other cities*--Colon City (34,655), Colon district (206,553), David City (82,907), David District (144,858). Terrain: Mountainous (highest elevation Cerro Volcan Baru, 3,475 m. (11,468 ft.)); coastline 2,857 km. (1,786 mi.).

Climate: Tropical, with average daily rainfall 28 mm. (1 in.) in winter.

In: Progress in Panama
Editor: Charles Bolitno

ISBN: 978-1-62417-932-7

Chapter 1

PANAMA: POLITICAL AND ECONOMIC CONDITIONS AND U.S. RELATIONS*

Mark P. Sullivan

SUMMARY

With five successive elected civilian governments, the Central American nation of Panama has made notable political and economic progress since the 1989 U.S. military intervention that ousted the regime of General Manuel Antonio Noriega from power. Current President Ricardo Martinelli of the center-right Democratic Change (CD) party was elected in May 2009, defeating the ruling center-left Democratic Revolutionary Party (PRD) in a landslide. Martinelli was inaugurated to a five-year term on July 1, 2009. Martinelli's Alliance for Change coalition with the Panameñista Party (PP) also captured a majority of seats in Panama's National Assembly. Panama's service-based economy has been booming in recent years – with a growth rate of 7.6% in 2010 and 10.6% in 2011 – largely because of the ongoing Panama Canal expansion project, now slated for completion in early 2015.

The CD's coalition with the PP fell apart at the end of August 2011when President Martinelli sacked PP leader Juan Carlos Varela as Foreign Minister. Varela, however, retains his position as Vice President. Tensions between the CD and the PP had been growing throughout 2011, largely related to which party would head the coalition's ticket for the

* This is an edited, reformatted and augmented version of Congressional Research Service, Publication No. RL30981, dated November 27, 2012.

2014 presidential election. Despite the breakup of the coalition, the strength of the CD has grown significantly since 2009 because of defections from the PP and the PRD and it now has a majority on its own in the legislature. President Martinelli's strong approval rating diminished in the aftermath of his break with the PP in 2011, but has recovered recently. President Martinelli's has been criticized by civil society groups and political opponents for taking a heavy-handed approach toward governing and for not being more consultative. At times, strong public protests have resulted in President Martinelli backing away from unpopular policy initiatives. While Panama's next presidential election is not scheduled until May 2014, the country will be gearing up for the race in early 2013. Martinelli is not eligible to run since Panama's Constitution only allows for a president to return to power after two terms (10 years).

U.S. Relations

The United States has close relations with Panama, stemming in large part from the extensive linkages developed when the Canal was under U.S. control and Panama hosted major U.S. military installations. The current relationship is characterized by extensive counternarcotics cooperation; support to promote Panama's economic, political, and social development; and a bilateral free trade agreement (FTA) that entered into force at the end of October 2012. U.S. bilateral assistance amounted to $3 million in FY2011 and an estimated $2.8 million for FY2012 while the FY2013 request is for $3.7 million. This funding does not include health assistance to combat HIV/AIDS and malaria funded under regional programs or assistance allocated to Panama under the Central America Regional Security Initiative (CARSI) that assists countries in their efforts to combat drug trafficking and organized crime. A number of U.S. agencies provide additional support to Panama.

The United States and Panama signed the bilateral FTA in June 2007, and Panama's National Assembly approved the agreement in July 2007. After more than four years, the U.S. Congress considered and approved FTA implementing legislation, H.R. 3079, on October 12, 2011, which President Obama signed into law on October 21, 2011 (P.L. 112-43). U.S. Congressional concerns had included Panama's labor rights and tax transparency issues, but the Obama Administration worked with Panama to resolve concerns over these issues. After the FTA was approved by both countries, work began on the implementation of the agreement over the next year. The agreement entered into force on October 31, 2012, after both countries had completed a thorough review of their respective laws and regulations needed for FTA implementation.

RECENT DEVELOPMENTS

On October 31, 2012, the U.S.-Panama Free Trade Agreement (FTA) entered into force. Both houses of Congress had approved implementing legislation for the FTA in October 2011, and the measure was signed into law by President Obama on October 21, 2011 (H.R. 3079, P.L. 112-43). (See "U.S. Commercial Relations and the Free Trade Agreement" below.)

On October 28, 2012, President Martinelli promulgated legislation repealing a recently enacted law initiated by his Administration that would have sold off state-owned land in the Colón Free Zone. Protests against the law resulted in three dead in clashes with the police. (See "Challenges for the Martinelli Government" below.)

From August 6-17, 2012, the United States and 16 nations from the region participated in annual PANAMAX defense exercises focused on ensuring the security of the Panama Canal. The exercises have been held annually since 2003. (See "Port Security and Other Counterterrorism Efforts" below.)

On July 31, 2012, the State Department issued its *Country Reports on Terrorism 2011*, which maintained that "the most direct terrorism threat to Panama" was the presence of a small unit of the Revolutionary Armed Forces of Colombia (FARC) in the Darién province bordering Colombia. Panama government has stepped up its efforts in recent years to confront this presence and has cooperated closely with Colombia to secure its border. The report maintained that Panama had an adequate legal and regulatory framework for countering terrorist finance, but also contended that "uneven enforcement of the existing anti-money laundering and terrorist finance controls...coupled with the weak judicial system, remained a problem." (The "Western Hemisphere Overview" section of the State Department's 2011 terrorism report is available at http://www.state.gov/j/ct/rls/crt/2011/195546.htm. Also see "Port Security and Other Counterterrorism Efforts" below.)

On May 24, 2012, the State Department issued its 2011 human rights report. According to the report, the Panamanian government generally respects human rights, but, remaining problems included harsh prison conditions, judicial ineffectiveness, and discrimination against various groups (especially indigenous groups) and individuals, including some cases of violence. The State Department reported that the judiciary was susceptible to corruption and outside influence and faced allegations of manipulation of power by other government branches, but also cited Panamanian government efforts to improve the functioning of the judiciary. (See “Human Rights Issues” below. The Panama section of the State Department human rights report is available at http://www.state.gov/documents/organization/186743.pdf.)

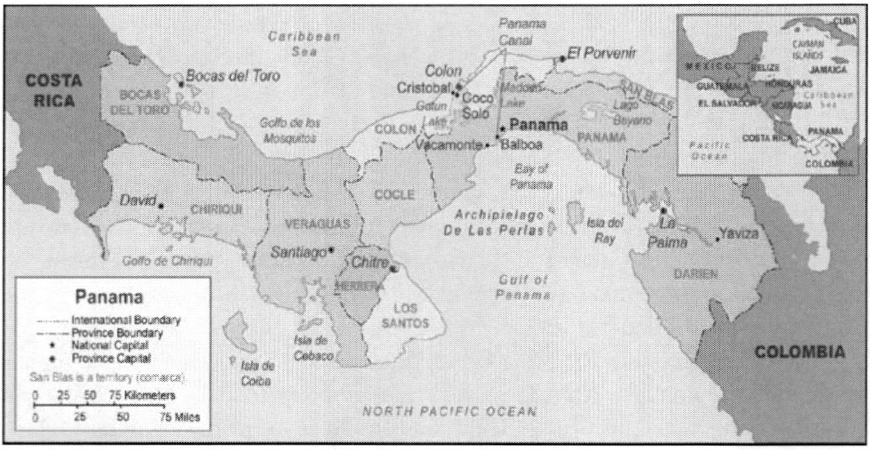

Source: Map Resources. Adapted by CRS.

Figure 1. Map of Panama.

POLITICAL AND ECONOMIC CONDITIONS

Panama has made notable political and economic progress since the December 1989 U.S. military intervention that ousted the military regime of General Manuel Antonio Noriega from power. The intervention was the culmination of two and a half years of strong U.S. pressure against the de facto political rule of Noriega, commander of the Panama Defense Forces. Since that time, the country has had five successive civilian governments, with the current government of President Ricardo Martinelli of the center-right Democratic Change (CD) party elected in May 2009 to a five-year term. Inaugurated on July 1, 2009, Martinelli is a businessman and former government minister. His electoral alliance, known as the Alliance for Change, also won a majority of seats in the unicameral National Assembly. Panama’s largely service-based economy has been booming in recent years, spurred on by the Panama Canal expansion project that begun in 2007 that is expected to be completed in 2015.

From the Endara to the Torrijos Administration

Endara Government (1989-1994)

Before the U.S. intervention, Panama had held national elections in May 1989, and in the presence of a large number of international observers, the anti-Noriega coalition, headed by Guillermo Endara, prevailed by a three-to-one margin. The Noriega regime annulled the election, however, and held on to power. By the fall, the military regime was losing political power and relied increasingly on irregular paramilitary units, making the country unsafe for U.S. forces and U.S. citizens. On December 20, 1989, President George H. W. Bush ordered the U.S. military into Panama "to safeguard the lives of Americans, to defend democracy in Panama, to combat drug trafficking, and to protect the integrity of the Panama Canal Treaty." Noriega was arrested on January 3, 1990, and brought to the United States to stand trial on drug trafficking charges. (Also see "Status of Manuel Noriega," below.)

As a result of the intervention, the opposition coalition headed by Guillermo Endara that had won the May 1989 election was sworn into office. During his term, President Endara made great progress in restoring functioning political institutions after 21 years of military-controlled government, and under his administration, a new civilian Public Force replaced Noriega's Panama Defense Forces. But Endara had difficulties in meeting high public expectations, and the demilitarization process was difficult, with some police and former military members at times plotting to destabilize, if not overthrow, the government.

Pérez Balladares Government (1994-1999)

In May 1994, Panamanians went to the polls to vote in presidential and legislative elections that observers called the freest in almost three decades. Ernesto Pérez Balladares, candidate of the former pro-Noriega Democratic Revolutionary Party (PRD), who led a coalition known as "United People," won with 33% of the vote. Placing a surprisingly strong second, with 29% of the vote, was the Arnulfista Party (PA) candidate, Mireya Moscoso de Gruber, heading a coalition known as the "Democratic Alliance."

In the electoral race, Pérez Balladares campaigned as a populist and advocated greater social spending and attention to the poor. He stressed the need for addressing unemployment, which he termed Panama's fundamental problem. Pérez Balladares severely criticized the Endara government for corruption, and he was able to overcome attempts to portray him as someone closely associated with General Noriega. (Pérez Balladares served as campaign manager during the 1989 elections for candidate Carlos Duque, who the Noriega regime had tried to impose on the electorate through fraud.) Instead, Pérez Balladares focused on the PRD's ties to the populist policies of General Omar Torrijos, whose 12-year (1969-1981) military rule of Panama ended when he died in a plane crash in 1981.

President Pérez Balladares implemented an economic reform program that included liberalization of the trade regime, privatization of state-owned enterprises, the institution of fiscal reform, and labor code reform. Tariffs were reduced to an average of 8%.

Pérez Balladares also worked closely with the United States as the date of the Panama Canal turnover approached. Under his government, Panama and the United States held talks on the potential continuation of a U.S. military presence in Panama beyond the end of 1999 (the date Panama was to assume responsibility for defending the Canal). Ultimately negotiations ended without such an agreement.

Although Panama's constitution does not allow for presidential reelection, President Pérez Balladares actively sought a second term in 1999. In 1997, the PRD had begun studying the possibility of amending the constitution to allow a second bid for the presidency in the May 1999 elections. Ultimately, a referendum was held on the issue in August 1998 but failed by a large margin.

Late in his administration, Pérez Balladares became embroiled in a scandal involving the illegal sale of visas to Chinese immigrants attempting to enter the United States via Panama. As a result, U.S. officials cancelled the former president's U.S. tourist visa in November 1999.[1]

Moscoso Government (1999-2004)

In her second bid for the presidency, Arnulfista Party (PA) candidate Mireya Moscoso was victorious in the May 1999 elections. Moscoso, who was inaugurated September 1, 1999, for a five-year term, captured almost 45% of the vote and soundly defeated the ruling PRD's candidate Martin Torrijos (son of former populist leader Omar Torrijos), who received almost 38% of the vote. Until March 1999, Torrijos had been leading in opinion polls, but as the election neared, the two candidates were in a dead heat. A third candidate, Alberto Vallarino, heading a coalition known as Opposition Action, received about 17% of the vote.

President Moscoso, a coffee plantation owner and Panama's first female president, ran as a populist during the campaign, promising to end government corruption, slow the privatization of state enterprises, and reduce poverty. She also promised to ensure that politics and corruption did not interfere with the administration of the Canal. The memory of her husband Arnulfo Arias, a nationalist who was elected three times as president, but overthrown each time, was a factor in the campaign, particularly since Arias was last overthrown in 1968 by General Omar Torrijos, the father of the PRD's 1999 and 2004 presidential candidate.

Although Moscoso took the presidency, the PRD-led New Nation coalition won a majority of 41 seats in the 71-member unicameral Legislative Assembly. Just days before her inauguration, however, Moscoso was able to build a coalition, with the support of the Solidarity Party, the Christian Democratic Party (which later became the Popular Party), and the National Liberal Party, that gave her government a one-seat majority in the Assembly. In August 2000, the Christian Democrats deserted the coalition and formed an alliance with the principal opposition, the PRD. However, corruption scandals in 2002 led to five PRD legislators defecting to support the Moscoso government, once again giving the president majority support in the Legislative Assembly.

The Moscoso government partially reversed the trade liberalization process of the Pérez Balladares by raising tariffs on some agricultural products, some of which reached the maximum rate allowed under Panama's World Trade Organization obligations.[2]

As noted above, Moscoso was elected as a populist, with pledges to end government corruption and reduce poverty, but her campaign pledges proved difficult to fulfill amid high-profile corruption scandals and poor economic performance. As a result, the president's popularity declined significantly from a 70% approval rating when she first took office in 1999 to only 15% in 2004.[3]

Torrijos Government (2004-2009)

In the May 2004 presidential race, Martín Torrijos of the PRD won a decisive victory with 47.5% of the vote, defeating former President Guillermo Endara, who received 30.6% of the vote, and former Foreign Minister José Miguel Alemán, who received 16.4% of the vote. Torrijos' electoral alliance also won a majority of seats in the unicameral National Assembly (formerly known as the Legislative Assembly), 43 out of 78 seats, which should provide him with enough legislative support to enact his agenda. Elected at 40 years of age, Torrijos—the son of former populist leader General Omar Torrijos (1968-

1981)—spent many years in the United States and studied political science and economics at Texas A&M University. He served four years under the Pérez Balladares government as deputy minister of interior and justice, and as noted above, became the PRD's presidential candidate in the 1999 elections.

Leading up to the election, Torrijos had been topping public opinion polls, with 42%-49% support. In the campaign, he emphasized anti-corruption measures as well as a national strategy to deal with poverty, unemployment, and underdevelopment. He was popular among younger voters and had a base of support in rural areas. Torrijos maintained that his first priority would be job creation.[4] He called for the widening of the Canal, a project that would cost several billion dollars, and would seek a referendum on the issue. During the campaign, all three major candidates supported negotiation of a free trade agreement with the United States, maintaining that it would be advantageous for Panama. Endara and Alemán appeared to emphasize the protection of some sensitive Panamanian sectors such as agriculture, while Torrijos stressed that such an agreement would make Panama's economy more competitive and productive.[5]

During his five years in office, President Torrijos faced such major challenges as dealing with the deficits of the country's social security fund (Caja de Seguro Social, CSS); developing plans for the expansion of the Panama Canal; combating unemployment, poverty, and increasing crime; and contending with the effects of the global financial crisis and U.S. recession on the Panamanian economy.

After protests and a protracted strike by construction workers, doctors, and teachers in June 2005, the Torrijos government was forced to modify its plans for reforming the social security fund. After a national dialogue on the issue, Panama's National Assembly approved a watered-down version of the original plan in December 2005. The enacted reform did not raise the retirement age but will gradually increase required monthly payments into the system and introduces a dual pension system that combines aspects of privatization with the current system.[6] In mid-December 2007, an almost six-week strike by doctors in the public healthcare system was resolved, with the government offering a 26.7% increase in salaries equivalent and a commitment not to privatize the system.[7]

In April 2006, the government unveiled its ambitious plans to build a third set of locks that would double the Canal's capacity, and allow larger post-Panamax ships to transit the Canal. Panama's Cabinet approved the expansion plan in June, and the National Assembly approved it in July 2006. A referendum on the expansion project took place on October 22, 2006, with

78% supporting the project. The referendum was viewed as a victory for the Torrijos government, which advanced the project as integral to Panama's future economic development and one that helped restore the president's popularity.[8]

The Torrijos government's agenda also included judicial, penal and anti-corruption reforms, as well as an economic development strategy to target poverty and unemployment. The government implemented a new penal code in May 2008 that took a tougher stance on crime by increasing sentences on serious crimes and other measures. In early July 2008, Panama's National Assembly gave President Torrijos powers to carry out security sector reforms over the next two months. In August 2008, President Torrijos enacted five decree laws reorganizing Panama's law enforcement and security services, including the establishment of a National Border Service and a National Intelligence and Security Service (SENIS). Some critics fear that the actions will lead to Panama's re-militarization, while Torrijos maintains that the new agencies are needed to combat growing drug crimes.[9] In mid-December 2008, the Torrijos government approved additional changes to the penal code that increased penalties for the illegal possession of firearms and introduced sentences for attacking a police official.[10]

In order to deal with the effects of the global financial crisis, President Torrijos announced the establishment of a $1.1 billion fund in January 2009 to allow for eased credit access and loans to financial institutions in Panama. The fund—financed with support from the Inter-American Development Bank, the Andean Development Corporation, and the National Bank of Panama— was established in order to counter the tightening of credit because of the global financial crisis.[11]

Martinelli Government (2009-2014)

May 2009 Elections

Because Panama's Constitution does not allow for immediate reelection, Torrijos was ineligible to run in the May 3, 2009, presidential election, which supermarket mogul and former government minister Ricardo Martinelli of the small center-right Democratic Change (CD) party won in a landslide. Despite strong economic growth and reductions in poverty, support for the Torrijos government in its last year in office eroded because of concerns about rising crime, the effects of the global financial crisis, and problems in improving infrastructure and public services. This contributed to the PRD's poor showing in the 2009 presidential and legislative elections.

While initially in 2008 it appeared that the candidate of the ruling PRD, former housing minister Balbina Herrera, was favored to win, opinion surveys late in the year reflected a significant shift in favor of Ricardo Martinelli. Polls in January 2009 showed Martinelli with 43% support compared to 25% for Herrera and almost 15% for Juan Carlos Varela of the center-right Panameñista Party (PP).[12] In late January 2009, Martinelli and Varela struck a deal to run together in a four-party coalition dubbed the Alliance for Change, with Martinelli leading the ticket and Varela as his running mate. The new alliance further widened Martinelli's lead in opinion polls. Ultimately, Martinelli captured 60% of the vote compared to almost 38% of the vote for Herrera.[13]

Martinelli's Alliance for Change also won a majority of seats in the unicameral National Assembly. The Alliance for Change parties captured 42 out of 71 seats in the legislature, with Martinelli's CD winning 15 and the PP winning 21 seats. The opposition PRD, however, remained the largest single party in the legislature, with 26 seats although internal divisions threatened to weaken its power.

Challenges for the Martinelli Government

The strength of President Martinelli's CD grew significantly after the 2009 election because of defections from other parties, but the CD's ruling alliance with the PP fell apart at the end of August 2011. President Martinelli sacked PP leader Juan Carlos Varela as Foreign Minister for allegedly neglecting his duties by spending too much time fostering his ambitions to run for President in 2014, while Varela maintains that the coalition fell apart because of policy differences related to transparency and accountability in the use of state resources.[14] Varela retains his position as Vice President, but plays the role of an opposition leader. Tensions within the coalition between the CD and the PP had been growing throughout 2011, largely related to which party would head the coalition's ticket for the 2014 presidential election. With the political realignment, initially the CD only had 33 seats in the 71-seat National Assembly, but three PP deputies switched to the CD and provided the President's party with a slim working majority of 36 seats. Subsequent defections from the opposition PRD provided the CD with a solid 40-seat majority in the National Assembly. [15]

President Martinelli's once strong approval rating diminished significantly in the aftermath of his break with the Panameñista Party in 2011, but has recovered recently. Between August and November 2011, his approval ratings dropped 20 points to almost 48%, and by May 2012, the President's approval rating, according to one poll, had dropped further to about 43%.[16] More recently, however, Martinelli's approval ratings have improved. A poll in September 2012 showed him with an approval rating of almost 58%.[17]

Nevertheless, at various junctures, President Martinelli has been criticized by civil society groups and political opponents for taking a heavy-handed approach toward governing and for not being more consultative and this has affected his popularity.

Some have criticized the President for undermining the independence of the judiciary. For example:

- In 2009, Martinelli nominated two political allies to the Supreme Court. A complaint on this and broader problems with Panama's judicial system was heard by the Inter-American Commission on Human Rights in March 2010, with representatives of the Citizens Alliance for Justice (Alianza Ciudadana Pro Justicia).[18]
- In April 2011, one of the Supreme Court justices appointed by President Martinelli resigned after accusations emerged that he had conspired to unseat former Attorney General Ana Matilde Gomez, who had been appointed by President Torrijos.[19] President Martinelli subsequently replaced the justice with an official who had worked at the Ministry of Economy and Finance as an acting deputy minister. His appointment elicited criticism because of a constitutional provision prohibiting someone from being a justice if they had worked in a position of authority (command or jurisdictional functions) in the executive branch of the current administration.
- In January 2012, Martinelli nominated two new Supreme Court justices to replace outgoing justices. While the nominations were approved by the National Assembly, some critics raised concerns that their appointment resulted in President Martinelli's increased influence over the judiciary.[20]
- In 2011, Panama's Supreme Court revived legislation originally approved in 1999 under the Pérez Balladares government that expanded the court from 9 to 12 judges and established a "court of constitutional guarantees" or fifth chamber within the Supreme Court. President Moscoso's government subsequently repealed the legislation expanding the court and the membership of the court returned to 9 members. But in January 2011, the Supreme Court

declared the Moscoso government's action unconstitutional so that the court could return to 12 members. Critics maintained that this would give President Martinelli even further influence over the court by having the ability to appoint three news justices or a total of 7 out of 12 justices on the Supreme Court.[21] In June 2012, however, strong public protests led President Martinelli to back down and withdrew his proposal for the fifth chamber.[22]

The President has backed away from other policy initiatives after strong public opposition. For example:

- In July 2010, Panama experienced labor unrest in response to controversial legislation that would have ended the obligatory payment of union dues and allowed companies to suspend contracts of striking workers and hire replacement workers during strikes. Two striking workers in the banana sector were killed in clashes with police in Bocas del Toro and hundreds were injured. The strike was suspended after the Martinelli government agreed to suspend some of the controversial aspects of the law. In October 2010, the government agreed to repeal the controversial labor provisions as well as provisions that would have relaxed environmental standards.[23]
- Protests by Panama's indigenous communities in early 2011 resulted in President Martinelli agreeing to repeal a controversial new mining law that would have facilitated foreign investment in the sector. Indigenous communities such as the Ngöbe-Buglé and others have opposed mining and hydroelectric projects in their territories. Continued indigenous protests in February 2012 over existing mining projects and a large planned hydroelectric project led to the death of two protestors, and resulted in the government making further concessions and engaging in talks with the indigenous communities. Protests reportedly could resume if the indigenous groups do not agree with the outcome of the talks.[24]
- In late October 2012, the Martinelli government agreed to repeal a recently enacted law that would have sold off state-owned land in the Colón Free Zone. Protests against the law resulted in three dead in clashes with the police. The government had argued that the revenue from the sale would be provided to the impoverished province of Colón, while opponents viewed the law as an attempt to conceal state spending and keep down the deficit.[25]

Economic Challenges

When the Martinelli government took office in 2009, it had to deal with the fallout stemming from the global financial crisis, but the economy weathered the storm and avoided the contraction experienced by many Latin American economies. Before the financial crisis, Panama's services-based economy had been booming, largely because of the Panama Canal expansion project, with the economy growing by over 10% in 2007 and 2008. The global financial crisis and U.S. recession slowed Panama's economic growth to 3.9% in 2009, but this still made Panama's economy one of the few in the region registering positive economic growth. Since then, the economy has rebounded, with a growth rate of 7.6% in 2010, 10.6% in 2011, and a forecast of 9.5% growth in 2012, fueled by both the Canal expansion project as well as the construction of a metro system in Panama City.[26]

Although Panama is categorized by the World Bank as having an upper-middle-income economy because of its relatively high per capita income level of $7,910 (2011), one of the country's major challenges is highly skewed income distribution with large disparities between the rich and poor. According to the U.N. Economic Commission for Latin America and the Caribbean, Panama's poverty rate was almost 37% in 2002, but declined to about 26% in 2009 and 2010. Extreme poverty or indigence in Panama also fell from 18.6% in 2002 to 11.1% in 2009, although it increased to 12.6% in 2010. In order to tackle poverty, the previous government of President Martin Torrijos (2004-2009) initiated a social support program of conditional cash transfers to poor families and the elderly living in extreme poverty. Since taking office, President Martinelli has fulfilled his campaign pledge to provide $100 a month to poor seniors. In May 2011, the World Bank approved a $100 million policy loan for Panama to help it strengthen fiscal management, improve tax collection, and expand key social programs.

The Martinelli government enacted two tax reform measures in 2010 that reduced corporate and personal income tax rates, and offset the loss of revenue by raising the sales tax from 5% to 7% (not including food) and raising other taxes on banks, casinos, airlines, and the free-trade zone, with a projected net increase in revenue. The government maintains that additional revenue from the reform will be used to augment social expenditures (such as scholarships and cash transfers to the elderly), although critics of the measure maintain that the poor will be hit by an increase in the cost of living. The measures prompted protests against the government, with violent clashes between police and demonstrators. The tax measure, however, also led to an upgrading of Panama's investment-grade credit rating.

In addition to the ongoing Panama Canal expansion project, the Martinelli government also initiated other infrastructure projects, including most significantly the building of an urban metro system for Panama City. Other projects include an expansion of Panama City's international airport and regional airports, a new bridge over the Atlantic side of the Canal, and highways, schools, and hospitals around the country.

Corruption

Concern about public corruption remains high in Panama. The World Economic Forum's report on global competiveness shows that corruption is viewed by business executives as the most problematic factor for doing business in Panama. According to the report, while Panama has improved its overall competitiveness, public trust in politicians is low and judicial independence is judged to be one of the lowest in the region. [27] President Martinelli has at times defended his cabinet ministers accused of corruption, while in other cases he has taken action to fire government officials or, in one case, let a minister resign on his own. Reports in Panama's press have chronicled allegations of corruption against government officials. In June 2011, the Martinelli government and the U.N Office on Drugs and Crime (UNODC) signed an agreement to establish a regional anti-corruption academy in Panama. According to UNODC, the academy will offer specialized courses to equip prosecutors, judges, police officers and other public officials with skills in the prevention, detection, and prosecution of corruption in public offices.

Crime

Another challenge for the Martinelli government has been dealing with crime, which increased significantly in 2008 and 2009. From 2000-2007, according to the UNODC, the annual homicide rate averaged about 11.1 1 homicides per 100,000 inhabitants, but subsequently increased to 19.2 100,000 in 2008 and 23.6 per 100,000 in 2009. In terms of numbers, Panama had 818 murders in 2009, a 25% increase over 2008, with drug trafficking reportedly the driving force behind the increase.[28]

During the 2009 electoral campaign, Martinelli proposed a safe streets program that included increasing the number of police and raising police pay. In February 2010, President Martinelli announced an expansion of the national police force with an additional 4,000 officers that would raise the total force to over 15,000.[29] According to the U.S. Department of State, efforts by the Panamanian National Police have had an impact on reducing crime.[30] The number of murders fell to 759 in 2010 (a decline of 8% from the previous year), according to UNODC.[31] In 2011, the number of murders continued to fall to a reported 704 homicides (almost a 7% decline), according to the U.S. Department of State, giving Panama a homicide rate of 19.3 per 100,000 for the year.[32]

Human Rights Issues

The Panamanian government generally respects human rights, but, as noted by the State Department in its 2011 human rights report (issued in May 2012), human rights problems continue in a number of areas. Among the principle problems cited were harsh prison conditions, judicial ineffectiveness, and discrimination against various groups (especially indigenous groups) and individuals, including some cases of violence. The State Department reported that the judiciary was susceptible to corruption and outside influence and faced allegations of manipulation of power by other government branches. It also noted, however, Panamanian government efforts to improve the functioning of the judiciary, including the implementation of a new code of criminal procedure (accusatory system of justice) in two provinces that should help speed up the administration of justice. The State Department also described some efforts by the government to improve prison and detention center conditions, including the establishment of a Penitentiary Training Academy to address human rights, prisoner rights, and penitentiary law.

Other human rights abuses, according to the State Department report, included problems with freedom of the press, trafficking in persons, and child labor.[33] For several years, successive Panamanian governments have used a variety of means to impede the media's freedom of expression. In January 2011, a draft law that would have allowed anyone convicted of insulting the president or an elected official to be sentenced to prison was withdrawn from consideration in the National Assembly after strong criticism by journalists and press rights groups.[34] Child labor violations reportedly occur most frequently in rural areas at harvest time and in the informal sector.

With regard to broader worker rights, the State Department notes that while Panamanian law recognizes the right of private-sector workers to form and join unions of their choice, the law requires a minimum of 40 persons to a form a union and only one trade union is allowed per business. The International Labor Organization (ILO) Committee of Experts criticizes both provisions as violations of workers' rights to organize. As noted above, Panama experienced labor unrest in July 2010 after the government approved legislation weakening labor laws in several respects, but the government subsequently repealed those provisions. In the lead up to the U.S. congressional approval of implementing legislation for the bilateral free trade agreement in 2011, Panama approved two new laws in April of that year that eliminated restrictions on collective bargaining for companies export processing zones, companies less than two years old, and companies in the special economic zone in the Barú region of Chiriquí province. (For more, see "Free Trade Agreement" discussion below.)

In February 2012, two protestors were killed during several days of clashes between police and indigenous protestors in Chiriquí province, while in late October 2012, three people were killed in clashes with police in the city of Colón during protests over a government proposal to sell state lands in the Colón Free Zone. In both cases, Amnesty International raised concerns about allegations of excessive use of force by security forces to disperse demonstrators. Similar concerns had been raised in July 2010 when two protestors were killed and hundreds of people injured in clashes with security forces during labor protests.

Over the years, violence from the civil conflict in neighboring Colombia has resulted in thousands of displaced persons seeking refuge in the neighboring Darién province of Panama. Many of the Colombians have lived in Panama for years, have given birth to children in Panama, and do not want to return to Colombia because of family and cultural ties to local Panamanian communities. According to the State Department's human right report, the Panamanian government restricts the movement of some 1,500 displaced persons Colombians in the Darién region covered under "temporary humanitarian protection." While the majority of the displaced are Afro-Colombians, there have also been indigenous people from Colombia who have fled to Panama because of the violence.

In addition to those under "temporary humanitarian protection," the State Department's notes that there were some 2,500 refugees and asylum seekers in Panama, while the Office of the U.N. High Commissioner for Refugees (UNHCR) classifies some 15,000 people in Panama as "persons of concern" in need of international protection. UNHCR has a permanent office in Panama that provides services to refugees.

2014 Presidential Election

While Panama's next presidential election is not scheduled until May 2014, the country will be gearing up for the race in early 2013. The

Democratic Revolutionary Party (PRD) is scheduled to hold a primary in early February 2013, with former mayor of Panama City Juan Carlos Navarro the favorite, and the Panameñista Party (PP) is scheduled to hold a primary in March 2013, with Vice President Varela the favorite. Martinelli's Democratic Change party has not announced the date of its party primary. Martinelli is not eligible to run since Panama's Constitution only allows for a president to return to power after two terms (10 years). There was speculation in the past about Martinelli wanting to amend the Constitution to allow for successive re-election, but this has been very unpopular in public opinion polls. Moreover, such a constitutional amendment was soundly defeated by a wide margin in a national referendum in 1998. Some observers maintain that President Martinelli might attempt to initiate a constitutional amendment to allow for re-election after one presidential term (five years).

U.S.-Panama Relations

Since the 1989 U.S. military intervention that ousted the regime of General Manuel Antonio Noriega from power (see "Background on the 1989 U.S. Military Intervention"), the United States has had close relations with Panama, stemming in large part from the extensive history of linkages developed when the Panama Canal was under U.S. control and Panama hosted major U.S. military installations. According to the Department of State, there are some 45,000 Americans in Panama at any given time, including tourists and those who reside in Panama, such as retirees of the former Panama Canal Commission and those who hold dual nationality. There are growing numbers of American retirees in the western part of the country in Chiriquí province.[35]

The current U.S. relationship with Panama is characterized by extensive cooperation on counternarcotics efforts; support to promote Panama's economic, political, and social development; and a bilateral free trade agreement (FTA) that was approved by Congress in October 2011and entered into force on October 31, 2012. Panama sought the FTA in order to make trade rules with the United States permanent, and perhaps more significantly, to promote increased foreign investment in the country. The United States has stressed that the FTA with Panama, in addition to enhancing trade by giving the United States greater access to Panama's growing market, would also provide greater access to Panama's large services market. According to the U.S. officials, Panama's strategic location as a major shipping route (with about 10% of U.S. international trade passing through the Canal), enhances the significance of the FTA for the United States.[36] Panama is currently in the midst of a $5.25 billion expansion of the Panama Canal, and has identified almost $10 billion in additional infrastructure projects in coming years that could provide opportunities for U.S. companies.[37]

The United States turned over control of the Canal to Panama at the end of 1999, according to the terms of the 1977 Panama Canal Treaty, at which point Panama assumed responsibility for operating and defending the Canal. All U.S. troops were withdrawn from Panama at that time and all U.S. military installations reverted to Panamanian control. However, under the terms of the Treaty on the Permanent Neutrality and Operation of the Panama Canal, or simply the Neutrality Treaty, the United States retains the right to use military force if necessary to reopen the Canal or restore its operations.

U.S. Foreign Aid and Other Support

Because of Panama's relatively high per capita income level, the United States has not provided large amounts of foreign aid to Panama in recent years. Nevertheless, aid has included development assistance to improve business competitiveness and trade-led economic growth; child, survival, and health assistance to help in the fight against HIV/AIDS and malaria; and security assistance to improve Panama's counterterrorism capabilities, border security programs, and maritime interdiction. U.S. bilateral assistance (not including Peace Corps) amounted to $3 million in FY2011 and an estimated $2.8 million in FY2012.

The FY2013 bilateral foreign aid request of $3.7 million for Panama is broken down into the following foreign aid accounts as follows: $2.8 million for Foreign Military Financing (FMF) to be used to train and equip Panama's National Border Service (SENAFRONT) and National Air-Naval Service (SENAN), provide spare parts for boats and communications equipment for maritime services, and procure vehicles for the Panama's Public Forces; $720,000 for International Military Education and Training (IMET) to support training and professionalization of Panama's Public Forces and civilian personnel involved in security-related duties; and $135,000 for Nonproliferation, Antiterrorism, Demining and Related Programs (NADR) assistance to strengthen the capacity of the Panamanian government to combat terrorist threats and secure its borders. (Congress has not yet completed FY2013 foreign aid appropriations legislation, but it approved a continuing appropriations resolution in September 2012 (H.J.Res. 117, P.L. 112-175) through March 27, 2013, at the same rate for projects and activities in FY2012, plus an across-the-board increase of 0.612%. It is unclear, however, how much Panama will be allocated under this legislation.)

This funding does not include two other types of assistance that Panama receives from U.S. centralized or regional programs. First, Panama some aid from U.S. regional programs implemented by the U.S. Agency for International Development (USAID) to combat HIV/AIDS and malaria. Second, Panama has been receiving significant amounts of assistance since FY2008 initially under the Mexico-focused Mérida Initiative and, beginning in FY2010, under the Central America Regional Security Initiative (CARSI) that assists countries in their efforts to combat drug trafficking and organized crime. While Panama was reported to have received an estimated $11 million under the Mérida Initiative for FY2008/FY2009, the Administration has not provided public information on how much each Central American country is receiving under CARSI.

Overall Central America funding for the Mérida Initiative/CARSI program amounted to almost $497 million from FY2008-FY2012, with another $107.5 million requested in FY2013.[38]

A number of U.S. agencies provide support to Panama. The Peace Corps has about 230 volunteers in the country working on a range of development projects. The State Department, the Drug Enforcement Administration, the U.S. Coast Guard, and the Department of Homeland Security are involved in providing counternarcotics support to Panama.

The U.S. Southern Command (Southcom) provides support to Panama through military exercises providing humanitarian and medical assistance, and at times provides emergency assistance in the case of natural disasters such as floods or droughts. Southcom has sponsored annual multinational training exercises since 2003 focused on the defense of the Panama Canal.

Panama hosts the Smithsonian Tropical Research Institute dedicated to studying biological diversity. Panama also participates in the Container Security Initiative (CSI) operated by the U.S. Customs and Border Protection of the Department of Homeland Security, and the Megaports Initiative run by the National Nuclear Security Administration of the Department of Energy. For many years, USAID had a mission in Panama administering U.S. foreign aid programs. Because of Panama's progress in economic development, USAID was able to close its Panama mission in September 2012, but will continue to provide support for some programs through its Central America Regional program based in El Salvador.

Port Security and Other Counterterrorism Efforts

Panama also participates in the Container Security Initiative (CSI) operated by the U.S. Customs and Border Protection of the Department of Homeland Security, and the Megaports Initiative run by the National Nuclear Security Administration of the Department of Energy. Three Panamanian ports—Balboa, Colón, and Manzanillo—participate in the CSI, while those three ports plus the port of Cristobal participate in the Megaports Initiative. The CSI uses a security regime to ensure that containers that pose a potential risk for terrorism are identified and inspected at foreign ports before they are placed on vessels destined for the United States. The Megaports Initiative involves deploying radiation detection equipment in order to detect nuclear or radioactive materials.

The State Department's *Country Reports on Terrorism 2011*, issued in July 2012, maintained that "the most direct terrorism threat to Panama was the persistent presence of small unit of the Revolutionary Armed Forces of Colombia (FARC)" in the Darién province bordering Colombia.[39] A small number of FARC members from the guerrilla group's 57th Front were reported to operate in the Darién, using the area as a safe haven. Panama's government has stepped up its efforts in recent years to confront this presence by patrolling the province and conducting raids against FARC camps. Panama has cooperated closely with Colombia to secure its border. President Martinelli stated in May 2012 that his country would soon have sovereignty over all its national territory because of its efforts to expel the FARC from Darien province.[40] In 2012, the government has continued to conduct raids on FARC camps in the region.

With regard to countering terrorist finance, the State Department terrorism report maintained that Panama had an adequate legal and regulatory framework for countering terrorist finance, although the report also contended that "uneven enforcement of the existing anti-money laundering and terrorist finance controls...coupled with the weak judicial system, remained a problem." The report also noted that the Colón Free Zone remained vulnerable to abuse for illicit finance.

With regard to the protection of the Panama Canal, the United States and Panama have continued to work together to plan for potential incidents that could close the Canal. Since 2003, Panama has participated in annual PANAMAX defense exercises with the United States and a number of other Latin American countries focused on ensuring the security of the Canal. The most recent exercise was held in August 2012 involving 17 nations in the region involving more than 1,000 military personnel.

Cooperation to Combat Drug Trafficking and Money Laundering

An important concern for U.S. policymakers over the years has been securing Panamanian cooperation to combat drug trafficking and money laundering. Panama is a major transit country for illicit drugs from South America to the U.S. market because of its geographic location and its large maritime industry and containerized seaports. The State Department's March 2012 *International Narcotics Control Strategy Report* (*INCSR*) maintains that Colombian and Mexican drug trafficking operations and a unit of the Revolutionary Armed Forces of Colombia (FARC) have used Panama's remote spaces (such as the Darién region bordering Colombia), its coastline and littoral zones, and its transportation infrastructure to move drugs through the country's territory. Panama's large financial sector and the Colón Free Zone (CFZ) also make the country vulnerable to money laundering. According to the *INCSR*, the majority of money laundering is believed primarily to be related to drug trafficking. The CFZ also reportedly continues to be vulnerable to abuse by criminal groups through illicit financial activities, largely because of insufficient enforcement of existing controls. (Also see further discussion of "Colón Free Zone" below.)

The State Department maintains that the Martinelli government is continuing Panama's history of close counternarcotics cooperation with the United States. Panama seized 34 metric tons of cocaine in 2011 compared to 49.5 metric tons in 2010. According to the State Department, the decrease is likely because of the disruption of established trafficking organizations, a shift in trafficking trends away from multi-ton shipments, and Panama's increased deployment of antidrug assets around the country.

Since 2009, the Martinelli government has established several air and naval anti-drug bases on both the Pacific and Caribbean sides of the country in an effort to increase the ability of its security forces to interdict suspected trafficking vessels.

In early October 2012, President Martinelli inaugurated the construction of the first of 19 radar systems that will cover both coasts of the country and form part of a strategy to deter and interdict drug shipments attempting to transit the country.

U.S. counternarcotics support has included programs to improve Panama's ability to intercept, investigate, and prosecute illegal drug trafficking; strengthen Panama's judicial system; improve Panama's border security; and promote strict enforcement of existing laws. The United States has provided resources to modernize, train, and maintain vessels and facilities of the National Air-Naval Service (SENAN), the National Border Service (SENAFRONT), the National Police (PNP), and the Ministry of Public Security; assisted with training and maintenance for aircraft involved in interdiction efforts; supported and encouraged a growing training program of Panama's security forces by Colombian police; and supported a law enforcement modernization project within the PNP.

In the March 2012 *INCSR*, the State Department encourages Panama to devote more resources to the modernization of its security and justice services, and maintains that Panama would be strengthened by a renewed focus on law enforcement modernization, anticorruption, strategic planning, judicial and prosecutorial reform, decentralization of decision making and a stronger focus on community-oriented policing.

Panama has made significant progress in strengthening its anti-money-laundering regime since June 2000, when it was cited as a non-cooperative country in the fight against money laundering by the Financial Action Task Force (FATF), a multilateral anti-money-laundering body. Subsequently, the government undertook a comprehensive effort to improve its anti-money-laundering regime by enacting two laws and issuing two decrees in 2000. As a result of these efforts, the FATF removed Panama from its non-cooperative country list in June 2001.

Panama has made progress over the past two years in improving the transparency of its financial system. It signed a Tax Information Exchange Agreement (TIEA) with the United States in November 2010, and by early July 2011 had signed enough tax agreements with other countries for the Organization for Economic Co-operation and Development (OECD) to remove the country from its so-called "gray list," a list of countries judged not to have implemented an internationally agreed tax standard. (Jurisdictions that have signed at least 12 such agreements for the exchange of tax information are considered by the OECD to have substantially implemented the tax standard and are removed from the list.)

It should be noted, however, that although Panama was removal from the OECD's "gray list," the country will still be subject to peer reviews of its legal and regulatory system for the exchange of information for tax purposes.

For a number of years, the State Department has expressed concern about Panama's use of bearer shares, often associated with money laundering, and maintained that the government should take steps to eliminate or immobilize these financial instruments. Panama took action on this issue on February 1, 2011, when President Martinelli signed into law bearer shares or "know your client" legislation. While Panama has made significant progress in improving its anti-money laundering regime, the State Department maintains in its March 2012 *INCSR* that the government's uneven enforcement and a weak judicial system susceptible to corruption and favoritism facilitates the work of money launderers.

Both the signing of a TIEA with the United States and Panama's approval of legislation related to "bearer shares" were issues raised by the United States in order to secure congressional approval of implementing legislation for the bilateral free trade agreement. (See "Road to U.S. Congressional Approval: Resolving Labor and Tax Issues" below.)

U.S. Commercial Relations and the Free Trade Agreement

Panama has a largely services-based economy, and has historically run a merchandise trade deficit with the United States. In 2011, the United States ran a $7.9 billion trade surplus with Panama, exporting about $8.2 billion in goods and importing $389 million. Panama's major exports to the United States include fish and seafood, gold, sugar, and fresh fruits. Major imports from the United States include oil, machinery, aircraft, consumer goods, and foodstuffs. The stock of U.S. foreign direct investment in Panama was estimated at $5.7 billion in 2011 (based on a historical-cost basis), led by the finance/insurance and wholesale trade sectors.

Until the bilateral free trade agreement (FTA) entered into force on October 31, 2012, Panama had been a beneficiary of specialized U.S. preferential import programs for Caribbean Basin nations for almost 28 years.[41] The Caribbean Basin Initiative (CBI) began in 1984 pursuant to the Caribbean Basin Economic Recovery Act (CBERA). The program was amended several times and was made permanent in 1990 in so-called CBI II legislation. CBI benefits were expanded in 2000 with the enactment of the Caribbean Basin Trade Partnership Act (CBTPA), which provided NAFTA-equivalent trade benefits, including tariff preferences for textile and apparel goods, to certain CBI countries, including Panama. In May 2010, Congress approved an extension of CBTPA benefits through September 2020 (P.L. 111-

171). With the FTA entering into force at the end of October 2012, its benefits replaced those for Panama under the CBERA, CBTPA, as well as broader U.S. trade preferences in the U.S. Generalized System of Preferences (GSP).

Free Trade Agreement

Panama and the United States began negotiations for a free trade agreement in April 2004. There had been expectations that the negotiations would be completed in early 2005, but continued contention over several issues and a lengthy hiatus prolonged the negotiations until December 2006. Issues included market access for agricultural products, considered sensitive by Panama; procurement provisions for the Panama Canal Authority regarding expansion activities; and sanitary control systems governing the entry of U.S. products and animals to the Panamanian market. Negotiations were suspended for some time in 2006 until after Panama held its Canal expansion referendum in October, but a 10th round led to the conclusion of negotiations on December 19, 2006. In December 2006, Panama and the United States also signed a bilateral agreement on sanitary and phytosanitary measures in which Panama recognized the equivalence of the U.S. food safety inspection to those of Panama and no longer required individual plant inspections.

When the FTA negotiations were concluded, then-U.S. Trade Representative Susan Schwab stated that the agreement would be subject to additional discussions on labor, and that the Administration would work with both sides of the aisle in Congress to ensure strong bipartisan support before submitting it to Congress.[42] On May 10, 2007, congressional leaders and the Bush Administration announced a bipartisan trade deal whereby pending free trade agreements would include enforceable key labor and environmental standards. This included an obligation to adopt and maintain in practice five basic internationally recognized labor principles: freedom of association; recognition of the right to collective bargaining; elimination of forced or compulsory labor; abolition of child labor; and elimination of discrimination in respect of employment and occupation.

The United States and Panama ultimately signed the proposed FTA on June 28, 2007, with the enforceable labor and environmental standards outlined in the bipartisan trade deal. Panama's National Assembly ratified the agreement on July 11, 2007, by a vote of 58 to 3, with one abstention. After more than four years, the U.S. Congress approved implementing legislation for the FTA on October 12, 2011 (P.L. 112-43).

After the FTA was approved by both countries, work began on the implementation of the agreement over the next year. On October 22, 2012,

U.S. Trade Representative Ron Kirk and Panamanian Minister of Commerce and Industry Ricardo Quijano exchanged letters determining that the agreement would enter into force on October 31, 2012. According to the Office of the United States Trade Representative (USTR), both countries completed a thorough review of their respective laws and regulations related to the implementation of the agreement.[43] In late September 2012, Panama's National Assembly had approved a package of final laws needed for FTA implementation, including laws related to the country's copyright and intellectual property rights regime, and President Martinelli signed the measures into law by October 10, 2012 along with an executive decree related to the way Panama administers its tariff-rate quotas. This cleared the way for the exchange of letters and for the FTA to enter into force.[44]

Under the FTA, over 86% of U.S. exports of consumer and industrial goods became duty-free when the agreement entered into force, while remaining tariffs will be phased out over 10 years. Almost 50% of U.S. agricultural exports to Panama became duty-free immediately, while tariffs on most remaining farm products will be phased out within 15 years. Under the FTA, U.S. companies are to be guaranteed a fair and transparent process to sell goods and services to Panamanian government entities, including the Panama Canal Authority. The agreement provides improved access to Panama's $22 billion services market, which includes financial, telecommunications, computer, express delivery, energy, environmental, and energy services. In addition to the $5.25 billion Canal expansion project, scheduled for completion in 2015, Panama has identified almost $10 billion in additional infrastructure projects in coming years that could provide opportunities for U.S. companies. [45]

For additional information, see the USTR's website on the U.S.-Panama FTA, available at http://www.ustr.gov/uspanamatpa.

Road to U.S. Congressional Approval: Resolving Labor and Tax Issues

The U.S. Congress had been likely to consider implementing legislation for the agreement in the fall of 2007, but the September 1, 2007, election of Pedro Miguel González of the ruling PRD to head Panama's legislature for one year delayed consideration of the FTA. González is wanted in the United States for his alleged role in the murder of U.S. Army Sergeant Zak Hernández and the attempted murder of U.S. Army Sergeant Ronald Marshall in June 1992. The State Department issued a statement expressing deep disappointment about the election of González because of his October 1992 indictment in the United States for the murder of Sergeant Hernández. Although González was acquitted in Panama in 1997 for the Hernández murder, observers maintain that the trial was marred by jury rigging and witness intimidation. González denies his involvement, and his lawyer asserts that ballistic tests in the murder were inconclusive. While polls in Panama in 2007 showed that Panamanians believed that González should have stepped down, the case also energized the populist anti-American wing of the ruling PRD.[46] González did not seek a second term as president of the National Assembly when his term expired on September 1, 2008, and another PRD official was elected Assembly president. This essentially removed the issue as an impediment to U.S. congressional consideration of the FTA, although implementing legislation was not introduced until the 112th Congress.

In order to secure congressional approval, the Obama Administration focused on working out final issues with Panama related to labor rights and tax transparency, and on April 18, 2011, United States Trade Representative Ron Kirk maintained that completion of action on these issues had cleared the way for technical discussions with Members of Congress on the draft implementing bill for the Panama FTA.[47]

The United States raised labor issues related to restrictions on collective bargaining rights in Panama's export processing zones (EPZs) and the right to strike in companies less than two years old. Legislation addressing both issues was approved by Panama's National Assembly in late March 2011 and signed into law by President Martinelli on April 5, 2011. The legislation eliminated restrictions on collective bargaining in EPZs and also eliminated the prohibition against the right to strike in companies less than two years old.

Another labor issue raised by the United States related to labor rights in a special economic zone in Panama's Barú region in the western province of Chiriquí. The law that had established the special zone made collective bargaining discretionary for six years.[48] In late March 2011, Panama's National Assembly approved legislation that extended full collective bargaining rights to workers in the special economic zone in Barú, and President Martinelli signed the measure into law on April 5, 2011.[49]

With regard to tax transparency issues, some Members of Congress had wanted to delay consideration of the Panama FTA until the United States and Panama signed a Tax Information Exchange Agreement (TIEA). This ultimately occurred on November 30, 2010. In a joint declaration at the signing of the TIEA, both countries agreed that the agreement would take effect as soon as practicable after Panama approves implementing legislation under its domestic laws to comply fully with the terms of the agreement. As noted in the declaration, Panama also maintained that it would enact legislation requiring the identification of the owners of bearer shares, an issue that U.S. officials have raised with Panama for a number of years.[50] Such legislation on bearer shares, also referred to as "know your client" legislation, was signed into law by President Martinelli on February 1, 2011. Panama's National Assembly subsequently approved the TIEA on April 13, 2011, and the measure was enacted into law and entered into force on April 18, 2011. According to the Treasury Department, the agreement provides the United States with access to information it needs to enforce U.S. tax laws, including information related to bank accounts in Panama. It permits both countries to seek information from each other on all types of national taxes in both civil and criminal matters for tax years beginning on or after November 30, 2007.[51]

Legislative Action on the FTA

Several measures were introduced early in the 112th Congress in support of the FTA with Panama. S.Res. 20 (Johanns), introduced January 25, 2011, would have expressed the sense of the Senate that the United States should immediately approve FTAs with Panama, Colombia, and South Korea. S. 98 (Portman), introduced January 25, 2011, would, among other provisions, expressed the sense of Congress that the President should submit the Panama, South Korea, and Colombia FTAs to Congress and that Congress should approve those agreements. H.Res. 86 (Frelinghuysen), introduced February 11, 2011, would have expressed the sense of the House that the Panama, Colombia, and South Korea FTAs should be implemented immediately.

Hearings were held in both houses in the 112th Congress on the proposed FTA with Panama. The House Ways and Means Committee held a hearing on the pending FTAs with Colombia, Panama, and South Korea on January 25, 2011.[52] A Senate Foreign Relations Committee minority staff report issued on February 8, 2011, urged the Administration to invest the political capital needed to secure approval of the Panama and Colombia FTAs.[53] The House Committee on Ways and Means, Subcommittee on Trade, and the Senate Finance Committee held respective hearings on February 9 and March 9 on the President's trade agenda featuring United States Trade Representative Ron Kirk. The House Committee on Foreign Affairs Subcommittee on the Western Hemisphere, held a hearing on the Colombia and Panama free trade agreements on March 17. The House Committee on Ways and Means, Subcommittee on Trade, held a hearing on the Panama FTA on March 30, 2011, featuring Deputy United States Trade Representative Miriam Sapiro and outside witnesses.[54] The Senate Finance Committee followed up with a hearing on the Panama FTA on May 25, 2011, that also featured the Deputy United States Trade Representative.[55]

Mock markups of draft implementing bills for the FTA were held on July 7, 2011, with the House Ways and Means Committee approving a draft bill along party lines by a vote of 22-15 and the Senate Finance Committee approving it by a vote of 22-2. Introduction of the final bill awaited congressional agreement on consideration of trade adjustment assistance (TAA) legislation.[56] Once the TAA issue was resolved, President Obama submitted implementing legislation for the Panama FTA on October 3, 2011 (H.R. 3079 and S. 1643). The House Ways and Means approved the measure on October 5, 2011 by a vote of 32-3 and the bill was reported on October 6, 2011 (H.Rept. 112-238), while the Senate Finance Committee reported its measure on October 11, 2011 without a written report. Both houses approved H.R. 3079 on October 12, 2011 (the House by a vote of 300-129 and the Senate by a vote of 77-22), and the President signed the measure into law on October 21 as P.L. 112-43.

Colón Free Zone

Panama's Colón Free Zone (CFZ), located at the Atlantic gateway to the Panama Canal, is the world's second largest free trade zone after Hong Kong. The vast trade volume that traverses the Panama Canal as well as Panama's modern financial sector and central location in the Americas make Colón a logical, if not ideal, place for a duty free zone. It serves as a "one stop shop" for both Latin American buyers and sellers from the rest of the world, including Asia and the United States. Sellers operate showrooms targeted at small- and medium-sized buyers, who make wholesale purchases of goods for retail sale in their respective countries. CFZ imports include a broad array of luxury goods, electronic products, clothing, and other consumer products, with Hong Kong the largest supplier and Colombia and Ecuador the largest destinations for CFZ exports.[57]

The U.S. Department of Commerce maintains that the CFZ offers a significant opportunity for U.S. retail companies to export to Latin America. According to the agency, U.S. companies can save time, grow sales, reduce complexity, and reduce financial risk by using the CFZ to export to the region.[58] The CFZ has its limitations, however, including that: it only covers consumer retail products (with no perishables and very little capital equipment); it is not suitable for exporting to larger countries such as Brazil and Mexico, which have their own internal buying structures; and some CFZ merchants should be avoided because of their poor reputation related to involvement in illicit activities.[59]

On this last point, the Department of State maintains that the CFZ is vulnerable to abuse by criminal groups through illicit financial activities, largely because of Panama's insufficient enforcement of existing controls. It maintains that a new electronic transaction recording information system for the CFZ will improve the capacity to trace transactions when the system is fully implemented.[60] (Also see "Cooperation to Combat Drug Trafficking and Money Laundering" above.)

Operation and Security of the Panama Canal

Historical Background and the Panama Canal Treaties

When Panama proclaimed its independence from Colombia in 1903, it concluded a treaty with the United States for U.S. rights to build, administer, and defend a canal cutting across the country and linking the Pacific and Atlantic oceans. (See Figure 1, "Map of Panama.") The treaty gave the United States rights in the so-called Canal Zone (about 10 miles wide and 50 miles long) "as if it were sovereign" and "in perpetuity." Construction of the Canal was completed in 1914. In the 1960s, growing resentment in Panama over the extent of U.S. rights in the country led to pressure to negotiate a new treaty arrangement for the operation of the Canal. Draft treaties were completed in 1967 but ultimately rejected by Panama in 1970.

New negotiations ultimately led to the September 1977 signing of the two Panama Canal Treaties by President Jimmy Carter and Panamanian head of government General Omar Torrijos. Under the Panama Canal Treaty, the United States was given primary responsibility for operating and defending the Canal until December 31, 1999. (Subsequent U.S. implementing legislation established the Panama Canal Commission to operate the Canal until the end of 1999.) Under the Treaty on the Permanent Neutrality and Operation of the Panama Canal, or simply the Neutrality Treaty, the two countries agreed to maintain a regime of neutrality, whereby the Canal would be open to ships of all nations. The U.S. Senate gave its advice and consent to the Neutrality Treaty on March 16, 1978, and to the Panama Canal Treaty on April 18, 1978, both by a vote of 68-32, with various amendments, conditions, understandings, and reservations. Panama and the United States exchanged instruments of ratification for the two treaties on June 16, 1978, and the two treaties entered into force on October 1, 1979.

Some treaty critics have argued that Panama did not accept the amendments, conditions, reservations, and understandings of the U.S. Senate, including the DeConcini condition to the Neutrality Treaty. That condition states: "if the Canal is closed, or its operations are interfered with, the United States of America and the Republic of Panama shall each independently have the right to take such steps as each deems necessary, in accordance with its constitutional processes, including the use of military force in the Republic of Panama, to reopen the Canal or restore the operations of the Canal, as the case may be." However, others argued that Panama, in fact, had accepted all U.S. Senate amendments. The State Department asserted that Panama expressly accepted all amendments, conditions, and understandings to the two treaties, including the DeConcini condition. The United States and Panama signed the instruments of ratification for both treaties, which incorporated all the Senate provisions. The two countries cooperated throughout the years on matters related to the Canal and established five binational bodies to handle these issues. Two of the bodies were set up to address defense affairs and conducted at least 16 joint military exercises between 1979 and 1985 involving Panamanian and U.S. forces.

Canal Transition and Current Status

Over the years, U.S. officials consistently affirmed a commitment to follow through with the Panama Canal Treaty and turn the Canal over to Panama at the end of 1999. That transition occurred smoothly on December 31, 1999. The Panama Canal Treaty terminated on that date, and the Panama Canal Commission (PCC), the U.S. agency operating the Canal, was succeeded by the Panama Canal Authority (ACP), a Panamanian government agency established in 1997.

Under the terms of the Neutrality Treaty, which has no termination date, Panama has had responsibility for operating and defending the Canal since the end of 1999. As noted above, both Panama and the United States, however, in exercising their responsibilities to maintain the regime of neutrality (keeping the Canal secure and open to all nations on equal terms) independently have the right to use military force to reopen the Canal or restore its operations. This is delineated in the first condition of the Neutrality Treaty.

The secure operation of the Panama Canal remains a U.S. interest since the Canal is important for U.S. ocean-borne trade. The Canal's largest trade route in FY2010 for ocean-borne cargo was between the east coast of the United States and Asia, which comprised almost 41% of total Panama Canal long tons cargo traffic. The Canal's second-largest trade route in FY2010 was between the east coast of the United States and the west coast of South America, which comprised almost 12% of total Panama Canal long tons cargo traffic. The United States provides assistance to Panama to improve its ability to provide security for the Canal and to enhance port and maritime security. U.S. officials have consistently expressed satisfaction that Panama is running the Canal efficiently, and since 2003, the U.S. military has conducted exercises with Panama and other countries to protect the Canal in case of attack.

Since the ACP has run the Canal beginning in 2000, it has been lauded for increasing Canal safety and efficiency. In September 2012, Jorge Luis Quijano was appointed by the ACP's Board of Directors to become the new Canal Administrator for a seven-year term, succeeding Alberto Alemán Zubieta who had served as Administrator since 1996. Quijano, an engineer, has worked at the Canal since 1975, and led the Canal expansion project beginning in 2006.

Canal Expansion Project

In April 2006, the Panama Canal Authority presented to then-President Torrijos its recommendation to build a third channel and new set of locks (one on the Atlantic and one on the Pacific) that would double the capacity of the Canal and allow it to accommodate giant container cargo ships known as post-Panamax ships. The project would also widen and deepen existing channels and elevate Gatun Lake's maximum operating level. The estimated cost of the seven-year project is $5.25 billion, to be self-financed by the ACP through graduated toll increases and external bridge financing of about $2.3 billion that would be paid off in about 10 years. According to the ACP, the overall objectives of the expansion project are to (1) achieve long-term sustainability and growth for the Canal's financial contributions to the Panamanian national treasury; (2) maintain the Canal's competitiveness; (3) increase the Canal's capacity to capture the growing world tonnage demand; and (4) make the Canal more productive, safe, and efficient.[61]

President Torrijos and his Cabinet approved the expansion project in June 2006, and the Legislative Assembly overwhelmingly approved it in July 2006, with 72 out of 78 deputies voting for the project. Pursuant to Panama's Constitution (Article 319), the project had to be submitted to a national referendum. The Torrijos government chose to hold the referendum on October 22, 2006, close to the anniversary of October 23, 1977, the date when Panamanians approved the two Panama Canal treaties in a national plebiscite by a two-to-one margin. The expansion project was approved by 78% of the vote, although there was some vocal opposition.[62]

The Panamanian government officially launched the expansion project on September 3, 2007, with a ceremony that included former President Jimmy Carter, whose Administration negotiated the Panama Canal Treaties. In March 2009, three multinational consortiums placed bids for the multi-billion dollar contract to build the new set of locks.[63] The ACP announced in July 2009 that the consortium *Grupo Unidos por el Canal* (United for the Canal) led by Spanish construction company Sacyr Vallehermoso was the winner of the contract after posting a bid of $3.12 billion. The consortium also includes Italian, Belgian, and Panamanian companies, as well as two U.S. companies—Montgomery Watson Harza and Tetra Tech—involved as design subcontractors.[64] In January 2010, the ACP awarded the fourth and final dry excavation contract to a consortium made up of Spanish, Mexican, and Costa Rican companies. The excavation work will create an access channel linking the new Pacific locks with the Gaillard Cut, which is the narrowest stretch of the Canal. While the project originally was expected to be completed by 2014, some delays reportedly have pushed the completion to April 2015.[65]

The Canal expansion is expected to reduce shipping rates between Asia and the U.S. Gulf and East coasts, resulting in significant savings and will likely increase Latin American trade with Asia as well as intra-Latin American trade. Many U.S. ports are already readying themselves in order to take advantage of the trade expansion. Some analysts maintain that the Canal expansion, which reportedly will allow 90% of the world's liquefied natural gas (LNG) tankers to pass through the Canal, will be a boon for the U.S. natural gas industry.[66] Others anticipate that the expansion will make U.S. Midwest grain exports more competitive in Asia.[67]

Background on the 1989 U.S. Military Intervention

The December 20, 1989, U.S. military intervention in Panama, known as Operation Just Cause, was the culmination of almost two and a half years of strong U.S. pressure, including economic sanctions, against the de facto political rule of General Noriega, Panama's military commander. Political unrest had erupted in mid-1987 when a high-ranking Panamanian military official alleged that Noriega was involved in murder, electoral fraud, and corruption, which prompted the formation of an opposition coalition that challenged his rule. The regime nullified the results of May 1989 national elections, which international observers maintain were won by the opposition by a 3-1 margin. It also harassed U.S. citizens in Panama, including the killing of a U.S. Marine lieutenant. President George H. W. Bush ultimately ordered U.S. forces into combat to safeguard the lives of Americans in Panama, to defend democracy, to combat drug trafficking, and to protect the operation of the Panama Canal.

In early January 1990, with the restoration of democracy and Noriega's arrest to face trial in the United States on drug charges, President Bush announced that the objectives of the U.S. intervention had been achieved. In terms of casualties, 23 U.S. soldiers and three U.S. civilians were killed, while on the Panamanian side, some 200 civilians and 300 Panamanian military were killed. While Congress was not in session during the intervention, in general, Members were strongly supportive of the action. In February 1990, the House overwhelmingly approved a resolution, H.Con.Res. 262, stating the President acted appropriately to intervene in Panama after substantial efforts to resolve the crisis by political, economic, and diplomatic means.

Status of Manuel Noriega

In the aftermath of the 1989 U.S. military intervention, General Manuel Antonio Noriega was arrested in January 1990 and brought to the United States to stand trial on drug charges. After a seven-month trial, Noriega was convicted on 8 out of 10 drug trafficking charges in U.S. federal court in Miami in 1992, and sentenced to 40 years in prison. That sentence was subsequently reduced to 30 years, and then to 20 years. With time off for "good behavior," Noriega was scheduled to be released from jail on September 9, 2007, but remained in U.S. custody pending appeals of his extradition to France. After exhausting his appeals, Noriega was extradited to France in April 2010. In France, Noriega faced a 10-year prison sentence for his conviction in absentia in 1999 on money laundering charges. He was eligible for a new trial upon his extradition to France, and in July 2010 was again convicted of drug money laundering and sentenced to seven years in prison.

On January 12, 2011, Panama requested Noriega's extradition from France for the 1989 killing of Major Moisés Giroldi, the leader of a failed coup in 1989. According to Panama's Ministry of Foreign Affairs, Panama previously had requested Noriega's extradition from France for the 1985 killing of vocal critic Hugo Spadafora.[68] Panamanian courts had sentenced Noriega to at least 60 years in prison for those offenses, although the law only allows him to serve a maximum sentence of 20 years, and according to some reports, his imprisonment in the United States and France could be subtracted from his sentence in Panama.

In November 2011, a French appeals court agreed to extradite Noriega, and he ultimately returned to his native country on December 11, 2011 and was imprisoned. In addition to his previous convictions in Panama, Noriega could face additional charges against him in Panama, including the 1970 disappearance and murder of labor activist Heliodoro Portugal. Noriega's return has not had any significant political fallout in Panama.

Since his return, the former military ruler has been hospitalized several times, most recently in November 2012. He has suffered two strokes and reportedly has heart disease, prostate cancer, and a benign brain tumor. Noriega's lawyers have requested that he be allowed to serve his time at home or in a medical center.[69]

APPENDIX. LINKS TO U.S. GOVERNMENT REPORTS

Background Note, Panama, State Department
Date: March 26, 2012
Full Text: http://www.state.gov/outofdate/bgn/panama/199022.htm

U.S. Relations with Panama, State Department
Date: October 24, 2012
Full Text: http://www.state.gov/r/pa/ei/bgn/2030.htm

Congressional Budget Justification for Foreign Operations FY2013, Annex: Regional Perspectives (pp. 827-829), State Department
Date: April 3, 2012
Full Text: http://www.state.gov/documents/organization/185015.pdf

Country Reports on Human Rights Practices 2011, Panama, State Department
Date: May 24, 2012
Full Text: http://www.state.gov/documents/organization/186743.pdf

Country Reports on Terrorism 2011 (Western Hemisphere Overview), State Department
Date: July 31, 2012
Full Text: http://www.state.gov/j/ct/rls/crt/2011/195546.htm

International Religious Freedom Report 2011, Panama, State Department

Date: July 30, 2012

Full Text:

http://www.state.gov/j/drl/rls/irf/religiousfreedom/index.htm?dlid=192991 #wrapper

International Narcotics Control Strategy Report 2012, Vol. I (Panama, pp. 355-359), State Department

Date: March 2012

Full Text: http://www.state.gov/documents/organization/187109.pdf

International Narcotics Control Strategy Report 2012, Vol. II (Panama, pp. 149-151), State Department

Date: March 2012

Full Text: http://www.state.gov/documents/organization/184329.pdf

National Trade Estimate Report on Foreign Trade Barriers 20112 (Panama)

Date: March 2012

Full Text: http://www.ustr.gov/webfm_send/2729

Trafficking in Persons Report 2012 (Panama, pp. 297-301), State Department

Date: June 19. 2012

Full Text:

http://www.ustr.gov/sites/default/files/NTE%20Final%20Printed_0.pdf

End Notes

1 "Ex-Leader of Panama Linked to Visa Sales," *Washington Post*, November 27, 1999; Pablo Bachelet, "U.S. Uses Visas to Combat Corruption," *Miami Herald*, February 21, 2006.

2 United States Trade Representative, *2006 National Trade Estimate Report on Foreign Trade Barriers*, p. 501.

3 "Toss Up Between Torrijos and Endara," *Caribbean and Central America Report*, February 17, 2004.

4 Frances Robles, "Ex-leader's Son Wins Presidency in Panama," *Miami Herald*, May 3, 2004.

5 "Panama: Presidential Candidates Remark on FTA with US," *La Prensa* (Panama), January 24, 2004, translated by Foreign Broadcast Information Service.

[6] Marion Barbel, "Panamanian Congress Approves Modified Social Security Reform," *World Markets Research,* December 22, 2005.

[7] "Panama: Country Report," *Economist Intelligence Unit* (EIU) January 2008, p. 2.

[8] Richard Lapper, "Good Luck, Good Timing," *Financial Times*, July 24, 2007.

[9] "Panama: Torrijos to Undertake Security Reform by Decree," *Latin American Weekly Report*, July 3, 2008; "Torrijos Forges Ahead with Security Decrees," *Latin American Regional Report, Caribbean and Central America*, September 2008.

[10] "Panama: Torrijos Pushes Through Changes to Penal Code," *Latin American Weekly Report*, December 18, 2008.

[11] Marion Barbel, "President Unveils U.S. $1.1 billion Anti-Crisis Fund in Panama," *Global Insight*, January 23, 2009.

[12] "Panama: Martinelli's Presidential Prospects Strengthen," *Latin American Weekly Report*, January 15, 2009, "Panama Mogul Extends Lead in Election Race – Poll," *Reuters*, January 11, 2009.

[13] Tribunal Electoral de Panama, "Elecciones Generales del 3 de mayo de 2009."

[14] "The Center for Strategic and International Studies and Inter-American Dialogue Hold a Discussion on Panama, Beyond the Canal," *Political Transcripts by CQ Transcriptions*, September 14, 2012.

[15] "Country Report: Panama," *Economist Intelligence Unit (EIU)*, December 2011 and October 2012.

[16] "Country Report: Panama," *EIU*, December 2011; and Louisa Reynolds, "President Ricardo Martinelli is Panama's Most Unpopular President, Says Recent Poll," *Noticen: Central American and Caribbean Affairs*, June 14, 2012.

[17] "Recupera Presidente de Panamá Apoyo de la Población," *Agencia Mexicana de Noticias (NOTIMEX)*, October 1, 2012.

[18] The Citizens Alliance for Justice represents 20 Panamanian civil society organizations dedicated to implementing judicial reform and improving the administration of justice. See the website of the alliance at http://www.alianzaprojusticia.org.pa/; The Washington, D.C.-based Due Process of Law Foundation has also done work on the issue of Panama's judicial system. For more information, see http://www.dplf.org/index.php?c_ID=395& catID=1.

[19] "Country Report: Panama," *EIU*, April 2011, p. 10.

[20] "Panama's Judiciary Under Opposition Scrutiny," *Latin News Daily Report*, January 4, 2012; "Panamá: Nuevamente el president contradice sus promesas con sus actuaciones," *La Estrella de Panama*, November 30, 2011.

[21] "Country Report: Panama," *EIU*, February 2011, p. 10.

[22] "New Alliance Claims First Victory," *LatinNews Daily Report*, June 21, 2012.

[23] Sean Mattson, "Panamanian President Ricardo Martinelli Reverses Course on Controversial Legislation," *Noticen, Central & Caribbean Affairs*, November 11, 2010; "Panama: Martinelli Performs Major U-Turn," *Latin American Regional Report, Caribbean & Central America*, October 2010.

[24] "Country Report: Panama," *EIU*, November 2012, p. 3.

[25] "Panama: Martinelli Performs another U-Turn," *Caribbean & Central America Report*, November 2012.

[26] "Country Report: Panama," *EIU*, October 2012.

[27] World Economic Forum, *The Global Competitiveness Report 2012-2013*, pp. 31, 33, and 286.

[28] United Nations Office on Drugs and Crime (UNODC), Homicide Statistics 2012, "Intentional Homicide Count and Rate per 100,000 Population (1995-2011)," available at http://www.unodc.org/unodc/en/data-andanalysis/homicide.html; "Panama: Drug-Fueled

Violence on the Increase," *Noticen, Central American & Caribbean Affairs*, January 28, 2010.

[29] "Panama Politics: President's Popularity Slips," *EIU ViewsWire*, March 23, 2010.

[30] U.S. Department of State, Bureau of Diplomatic Security, "Panama 2012 Crime and Safety Report," April 6, 2012.

[31] UNODC, op. cit.

[32] U.S. Department of State, "Panama 2012 Crime and Safety Report," op. cit.

[33] U.S. Department of State, "2011 Country Reports on Human Rights Practices, Panama," May 24, 2012, available at http://www.state.gov/documents/organization/186743.pdf

[34] "Withdrawal of Proposal to Introduce Jail Terms for Insulting the President," Reporters Without Borders, January 12, 2011.

[35] U.S. Department of State, Background Note: Panama, March 26, 2012.

[36] Office of the United States Trade Representative, Statement by Ambassador Miriam Sapiro, Deputy United States Trade Representatives, Statement before the House Committee on Ways and Means, Subcommittee on Trade, March 30, 2011.

[37] Office of the United States Trade Representative, "Benefits of the U.S.-Panama Trade Promotion Agreement," April 19, 2011.

[38] For additional information on CARSI, see CRS Report R41731, *Central America Regional Security Initiative: Background and Policy Issues for Congress*, by Peter J. Meyer and Clare Ribando Seelke.

[39] U.S. Department of State, *Country Reports on Terrorism 2011*, July 31, 2012, "Western Hemisphere Overview" section available at http://www.state.gov/j/ct/rls/crt/2011 /195546.htm

[40] "Martinelli Asegura Que Expulsará a las FARC de Región Fronteriza del Darién," *Agencia EFE*, May 31, 2012.

[41] Panama was not a beneficiary of the CBI from 1988-1989 when the United States was applying economic sanctions on the country during the rule of General Manuel Noriega.

[42] Rosella Brevetti, "Panama, United States Conclude Negotiations on Free Trade Pact," but Labor Issues Remain," *International Trade Daily*, December 20, 2006.

[43] USTR, "United States, Panama Set Date for Entry into Force of United States-Panama Trade Promotion Agreement," Press Release, October 22, 2012.

[44] Rosella Brevetti, "Officials Say U.S.-Panama FTA on Brink of Being Implemented," *International Trade Reporter*, October 11, 2012; "Panamanian Congress Advances Bills Required for FTA Implementation," *Inside U.S. Trade*, September 27, 2012; and "Panama Completes All Outstanding Steps for FTA Implementation," *Inside U.S. Trade*, October 11, 2012.

[45] Office of the United States Trade Representative, "Benefits of the U.S.-Panama Trade Promotion Agreement," April 19, 2011; USTR, "United States, Panama Set Date for Entry into Force of United States-Panama Trade Promotion Agreement," Press Release, October 22, 2012.

[46] Marc Lacey, "Fugitive from U.S. Justice Leads Panama's Assembly," *New York Times*, November 28, 2007.

[47] Office of the United States Trade Representative, "Ambassador Ron Kirk Announces Next Step for U.S.-Panama Trade Promotion Agreement," April 18, 2011. Also see White House, Office of the Press Secretary, "Fact Sheets: U.S.- Panama Trade Promotion Agreement," April 19, 2011, available at http://www.whitehouse.gov/the-press-office/2011/ 04/19/fact-sheets-us-panama-trade-promotion-agreement.

[48] "U.S. Focused on Labor Laws for New Panama Economic Zone," *Inside U.S. Trade*, February 17, 2011. Also see U.S. Department of State, "Country Reports on Human Rights Practices: Panama," April 8, 2011.

[49] Office of the United States Trade Representative, Statement by Ambassador Miriam Sapiro, Deputy United States Trade Representatives, Statement before the House Committee on Ways and Means, Subcommittee on Trade, March 30, 2011; and "Panama Moves Closer to Completing All Steps Necessary for FTA Vote," *Inside U.S. Trade*, April 1, 2011.

[50] U.S.-Panama Tax Information Exchange Agreement, Joint Declaration, November 30, 2010, available at http://www.treasury.gov/resource-center/tax-policy/treaties/Documents/Panama TIEAnote.pdf.

[51] U.S. Department of the Treasury, Press Release, "U.S., Panama Sign New Tax Information Exchange Agreement," December 1, 2010. See the full text of the TIEA, available at http://www.treasury.gov/resource-center/tax-policy/ treaties/Documents/PanamaTIEA10.pdf.

[52] See the witness testimony from the hearing, available at http://waysandmeans.house.gov /Calendar/EventSingle.aspx? EventID=220430.

[53] U.S. Congress, Senate Committee on Foreign Relations, *Losing Jobs and Alienating Friends: The Consequences of Falling Behind on Free Trade with Colombia and Panama*, committee print, 112th Cong., 1st sess., February 8, 2011, S. Prt. 112-?? (Washington: GPO, 2011), available at http://lugar.senate.gov/issues/foreign/lac/FTA.pdf.

[54] See the testimony of the March 30, 2011 hearing at http://waysandmeans.house.gov /Calendar/EventSingle.aspx? EventID=230458.

[55] See the statements of the May 25, 2011 Senate Finance Committee hearing, available at http://finance.senate.gov/ hearings/hearing/?id=fbdf8ce6-5056-a032-522a-f5ebc033b713.

[56] For background on TAA, see CRS Report R41922, *Trade Adjustment Assistance (TAA) and Its Role in U.S. Trade Policy*, by J. F. Hornbeck and Laine Elise Rover.

[57] U.S. Department of Commerce, U.S. Commercial Service, "Doing Business in Panama 2012," April 2012.

[58] U.S. Department of Commerce, U.S. Commercial Service, "Sell Through Panama's Colon Free Trade Zone to the Region –a U.S. Export Opportunity," May 2011.

[59] Ibid.

[60] U.S. Department of State, *International Narcotics Control Strategy Report, Volume II, Money Laundering and Financial Crimes*, March 2012, pp. 149-151.

[61] Autoridad del Canal de Panama (ACP), "Proposal for the Expansion of the Panama Canal, Third Set of Locks Project," April 24, 2006.

[62] Among the opponents, an organization known as the Peasant Coordinator Against the Dams (CCCE, *Coordinadora Campesina Contra los Embalses*), consisting of agricultural, civil, and environmental organizations, asserted that the expansion project would lead to flooding and would drive people from their homes. An umbrella protest group known as the National Front for the Defense of Economic and Social Rights (*Frenadeso*), which was formed in 2005 during protests against social security reforms, called for a "no" vote. "Torrijos Appeals for Approval of Canal Expansion," *LatinNews Daily*, September 1, 2006.

Former Presidents Jorge Illueca and Guillermo Endara, as well as former Panama Canal Administrator Fernando Manfredo, also opposed the expansion project, maintaining that the price was too high and too much of a gamble. Critics feared that the total price tag could rise considerably and expressed concern that toll increases could make alternative routes more economically attractive. Panama: Torrijos Reveals Plans to Expand Canal," *LatinNews Daily*, April 25, 2006; Chris Kraul and Ronald D. White, "Panama is Preparing to Beef up the Canal," *Los Angeles Times*, April 24, 2006; John Lyons, "Panama Takes Step Toward Expanding the Canal," *Wall Street Journal*, April 24, 2006.

[63] "Panama: Groups Bid on Canal Expansion," *Economist Intelligence Unit, Business Latin America*, March 9, 2009.

[64] "Unidos por El Canal Virtual winner of ACP contract," *Business News Americas*, July 8, 2009; and "Panama Canal Announces 'Best Value' Proposal for New Set of Locks Expansion Contract," *States News Service*, July 9, 2009.

[65] "Canal Progress Update," *Caribbean & Central America Report*, November 2012.

[66] Brian Hansen and Benno Spencer, "Panama Canal Expansion Could Be Boon for Budding U.S. LNG Export Industry," *Platts Gas Market Report*, August, 3, 2012

[67] Tim Johnson, "Canal Expansion to Alter Dynamics of Trade," *Seattle Times*, August 12, 2012.

[68] República de Panamá, Ministerio de Relaciones Exteriores, Comunicado de Prensa, "Extradición de Manuel Antonio Noriega por el caso Giroldi," January 12, 2011.

[69] "Panama's Noriega Back in Jail after Hospital Stint," *Agence France Presse*, October 12, 2012; "Noriega Va de Nuevo al Hospital para Examen Programado de Urología," *Agence France Presse*, November 21, 2012.

In: Progress in Panama
Editor: Charles Bolitno

ISBN: 978-1-62417-932-7

Chapter 2

THE U.S.-PANAMA FREE TRADE AGREEMENT*

J. F. Hornbeck

SUMMARY

On June 28, 2007, the United States and Panama signed a free trade agreement (FTA) after two and a half years and 10 rounds of negotiations. Negotiations formally concluded on December 16, 2006, with an understanding that changes to labor, environment, and intellectual property rights chapters would be made pursuant to future congressional input. These changes were agreed to and the FTA was signed in time to be considered under Trade Promotion Authority (TPA) legislation, which expired on July 1, 2007. TPA allows Congress to consider certain trade agreement implementing bills under expedited procedures. Panama's legislature ratified the FTA 58 to 4 on July 11, 2007, but neither the 110th nor the 111th Congress took up the agreement.

Eventually, the 112th Congress considered the FTA implementing bill. On July 7, 2011, the House Ways and Means and Senate Finance Committees held simultaneous "mock markups," where they informally approved draft implementing bills. On October 3, 2011, the Obama Administration transmitted final implementing legislation and supporting documents to both houses, as required under TPA. Following committee

* This is an edited, reformatted and augmented version of RL32540, Publication No. Congressional Research Service, dated November 8, 2012.

action, on October 12, 2011, the House agreed to the implementing bill (H.R. 3079) 300-129, followed by the Senate 77-22.

President Obama signed the implementing bill into law on October 21, 2011 (P.L. 112-43, 125 Stat. 427), but the FTA would not enter into force for another year. Panama required that time to complete changes in law necessary to bring it into compliance with the provisions of the FTA. On October 22, 2012, the United States Trade Representative (USTR) exchanged notes with Panama providing for entry into force of the FTA. President Obama implemented the agreement by proclamation on October 29, 2012, and the FTA entered into force on October 31, 2012.

The U.S.-Panama FTA is a comprehensive and reciprocal trade agreement, replacing U.S. unilateral preferential trade treatment extended under the Caribbean Basin Economic Recovery Act (CBERA), the Caribbean Basin Trade Partnership Act (CBTPA), and the Generalized System of Preferences (GSP). Some 88% of U.S. commercial and industrial exports will become duty-free upon implementation, with remaining tariffs phased out over a 10-year period. Over 50% of U.S. farm exports to Panama also will achieve immediate duty-free status, with tariffs and tariff rate quotas (TRQs) on select farm products to be phased out by year 17 of the agreement (year 20 for rice). The FTA also consummates understandings on telecommunications, services trade, government procurement, investment, and intellectual property rights.

The final text of the U.S.-Panama FTA incorporates changes based on the bipartisan agreement of May 10, 2007, crafted by the Bush Administration and leadership in the 110th Congress. These include adoption of enforceable labor standards, compulsory membership in multilateral environmental agreements, and an easing of restrictions on developing country access to generic drugs, provisions that go beyond those in previous U.S. bilateral FTAs and multilateral trade rules. Concerns raised in Congress on labor and tax transparency issues were also addressed by Panama in statute and by ratification of a Tax Information and Exchange Agreement (TIEA) with the United States. The TIEA provides greater tax transparency in support of curbing illicit financial transactions associated with money laundering activities.

This report covers issues related to the U.S.-Panama FTA from the beginning of the negotiations in April 2004 until the FTA entered into force on October 31, 2012.

INTRODUCTION

On June 28, 2007, the United States and Panama signed a free trade agreement (FTA) after two and a half years and 10 rounds of negotiations. The U.S.-Panama FTA is a reciprocal and comprehensive trade agreement, replacing U.S. unilateral preferential trade treatment extended under the Caribbean Basin Economic Recovery Act (CBERA), the Caribbean Basin Trade Partnership Act (CBTPA), and the Generalized System of Preferences (GSP). Negotiations formally concluded on December 16, 2006, with an understanding that changes to environment, labor, and intellectual property rights chapters would be made pursuant to future congressional input. These changes were agreed to and the FTA was signed in time to be considered under Trade Promotion Authority (TPA) legislation, which expired on July 1, 2007. TPA allows Congress to consider certain trade agreement implementing bills under expedited procedures.[1]

Panama's legislature ratified the FTA 58 to 4 on July 11, 2007 (see Appendix A for Chronology of U.S.-Panama FTA Milestones), but neither the 110th nor the 111th Congress took up the agreement. The 112th Congress considered the implementing bill when congressional leaders and the Obama Administration came to an understanding on how to proceed. On July 7, 2011, the House Ways and Means and Senate Finance Committees held simultaneous "mock markups," where they informally approved draft implementing bills. On October 3, 2011, the Administration transmitted to both houses of Congress final implementing legislation and supporting documents, as required under TPA.[2] Following committee action, on October 12, 2011, the House agreed to the implementing bill (H.R. 3079) 300-129, followed by the Senate 77-22.

President Obama signed the implementing bill into law on October 21, 2011 (P.L. 112-43, 125 Stat. 427), but the FTA would not enter into force for another year. Panama required that time to complete changes in law necessary to bring it into compliance with the provisions of the FTA. On October 22, 2012, the United States Trade Representative (USTR) exchanged notes with Panama providing for entry into force of the FTA. President Obama implemented the agreement by proclamation on October 29, 2012, and the FTA entered into force on October 31, 2012. This report discusses issues surrounding the U.S-Panama free trade agreement from the time formal negotiations began in April 2004 until it entered into force.

U.S. CONGRESSIONAL ACTION

Congress delayed action on the U.S.-Panama FTA for nearly four years because of numerous concerns. Many issues were addressed by changes to the FTA based on principles outlined in the bipartisan agreement of May 10, 2007, crafted jointly by leadership in the 110th Congress and the Bush Administration. These changes included adoption as fully enforceable commitments, the five basic labor rights defined in the International Labor Organization's (ILO's) *Fundamental Principles and Rights at Work and its Follow-up (1998) Declaration*, compulsory adherence to select multilateral environmental agreements, new pharmaceutical intellectual property rights provisions intended to facilitate Panama's access to generic drugs, and language on the investor-state issue clarifying that foreign investors will have no greater rights than U.S. domestic investors with respect to dispute resolution under the FTA.[3]

Other issues, however, cropped up that further hindered congressional action on the agreement, all falling outside the scope of the FTA. Soon after the May 10th understanding was agreed to, the election of Pedro Miguel González Pinzón as president of Panama's National Assembly on September 3, 2007, contributed to another year of delay.[4] Although a deputy in the National Assembly since 1999, his election to the head of the National Assembly raised his profile and drew the attention of Congress to his alleged role in the June 1992 murder of a U.S. serviceman in Panama. A Panamanian court acquitted him of the charge in 1997, but the United States does not recognize the verdict and maintains an outstanding warrant for his arrest.[5] This issue was effectively resolved with respect to the FTA on September 1, 2008, when González Pinzón declined to run for a second term as president of the National Assembly.

Labor Code Amendments

Despite the FTA's inclusion of labor principles based on the May 10th agreement, the 112th Congress raised concerns over four other specific labor statutes. First, the labor code prohibited Panamanian workers from striking against companies that had been in business for less than two years. Second, export processing zones were covered by separate labor provisions with more restrictive collective bargaining and right to strike language compared to the national labor code. Third, Panama, in creating the Barú Special Economic Zone, allowed firms there to (1) have a six-year moratorium on collective bargaining rights and (2) an extension from two to three years in the use of temporary workers. The National Assembly repealed these statutes in legislation passed in April 2011.[6] A fourth labor issue involved the statutory limitation on the minimum number of workers required to start a union.

Panama requires 40; the ILO recommends 20. This issue has been highlighted by the State Department and some Members of Congress.[7] The Panamanian government did not act on the so-called "40/20 Issue" for lack of support by business, government, or labor constituencies in Panama.

Tax Transparency

Historically, the United States has had an ongoing concern over problems with drug trafficking and money laundering through Panama, and critics have pointed to the need for greater tax transparency to help monitor and control related illicit financial transactions.[8] Panama was placed on the so-called "Gray List" maintained by the Organization of Economic Cooperation and Development (OECD), which includes jurisdictions that have committed to an internationally agreed tax standard, but have yet to implement it.[9] The Government Accountability Office (GAO) also listed Panama as one of 50 countries described as having "tax havens" or "financial privacy jurisdictions" according to a number of international organizations, and Panama had declined to enter into any agreements for the exchange of tax information.[10]

Although this issue falls outside the purview of the FTA, some Members of Congress and the Obama Administration wanted to delay consideration of the FTA until Panama signed a Tax Information and Exchange Agreement (TIEA) with the United States, and took other measures necessary to be removed from the OECD "Gray List," including implementing tax agreements with a minimum of 12 other countries.[11]

Panama and the United States came to a resolution on the tax transparency issue by agreeing to a TIEA, which Panama ratified on April 13, 2011. The TIEA permits either country to request information on most types of federal (U.S.) or national (Panama) taxes. To address the tax haven issue, Article 7 specifically allows for tax information exchange "under the existing Treaty on Mutual Legal Assistance in Criminal Matters," which covers money laundering among other illicit financial activities.

To address the "Gray List" issue, Panama also entered into 14 double taxation agreements in addition to the TIEA with the United States. Twelve of these agreements were ratified prior to congressional action on the FTA, and Panama was formally removed from the OECD "Gray List" on July 6, 2011.[12] Unlike the TIEA, the purpose of the double taxation agreements is to eliminate double national taxation in addition to taking on obligations of tax information and exchange, as set out by the OECD international tax standard.

Final Congressional Action

At the beginning of the 112th Congress, consideration of FTA implementing bills for Colombia, Panama, and South Korea became part of a larger trade legislative agenda that included reauthorization of trade adjustment assistance (TAA) programs. Two issues had to be resolved if legislation were to move forward. First, Congress had to write a TAA bill that would garner sufficient bipartisan support in both houses. Second, because of strong differences of opinion and increasing distrust between legislative and executive branches, a legislative path was needed that would ensure passage of all three implementing bills and the TAA legislation, in tandem.[13] An agreement was struck on a compromise TAA bill that both parties and houses of Congress eventually came to embrace.[14]

To address myriad concerns over assured passage of all four bills, congressional leaders and the White House agreed to an elaborate, fast-paced, and nuanced legislative process. The House began, passing a bill to reauthorize the Generalized System of Preferences (H.R. 2832), which was then sent to the Senate. The Senate amended the bill with the addition of TAA reauthorization. On September 22, 2011, the Senate agreed to the amended bill, 70-27, after which it was sent to the House.[15] In separate action, President Obama sent the three FTA implementing bills to both houses of Congress to be considered under rules provided in TPA. The House Ways and Means Committee favorably reported out all three FTA implementing bills on October 3, 2011. On October 6, 2011, the House Committee on Rules issued a closed rule covering all four bills.[16] The U.S.-Panama FTA implementing bill was agreed to by both houses along with the other three trade bills on October 12, 2011. President Obama signed the bill into law on October 21, 2012 (P.L. 112-43). After Panama completed legislative action necessary to bring Panamanian law into compliance with the agreement, the United States implemented the FTA by presidential proclamation, and it entered into force on October 31, 2012.

Panama's Canal and Economic Relations with the United States

The United States and Panama have entered into many agreements over the past 150 years, the most prominent ones defining their relative stakes in the canal that traverses the Central American isthmus, bisecting Panamanian territory. The canal has been a critical factor influencing Panamanian domestic and foreign affairs, and like earlier U.S.-Panama agreements, the FTA's significance is tied to a Panamanian economy that has formed largely around the canal.

Early U.S.-Panama Economic Relations

Since first explored by the Spanish at the turn of the 16th century, interest in Panama has centered on its unique geographic characteristic: the slender distance separating the Atlantic and Pacific Oceans (see Figure 1). Because of the transit possibilities this presented (first for Peruvian gold and other colonial trade), Panama was a natural crossroads for the movement of commerce, a strategic position that grew as the world became ever more traveled and integrated. In fact, Panama's destiny became fused to its geography and the foreign interests that sought to take advantage of it, particularly the United States.

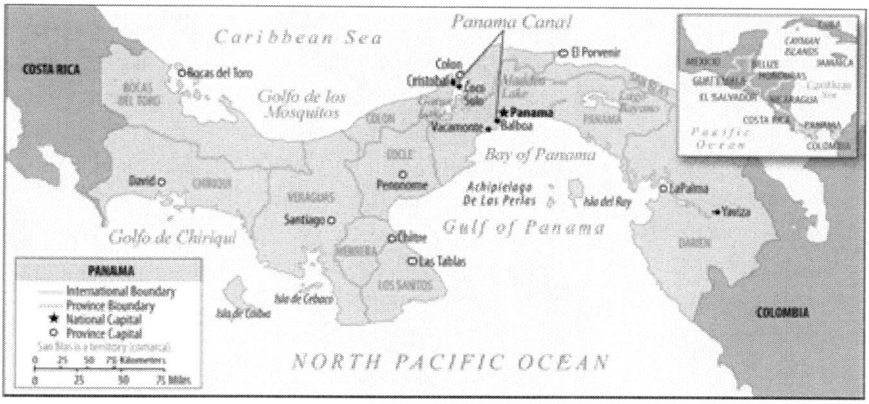

Source: CRS.

Figure 1. Map of Panama.

Panama was swept to independence from Spain on November 28, 1821, becoming part of the Gran Colombia regional group. By this point, both the United States and Britain had openly coveted the prospect of an inter-oceanic connector. Well before construction of a canal could begin, the United States displaced Britain as the dominant foreign influence and completed a cross-isthmian railroad in 1855. This project was driven by the westward expansion of the United States, which included an anticipated southern water route to the west coast. To secure this transit system, as well as the safety of goods and people using it, the United States resorted to armed intervention in Panama some 14 times in the 19th century. By the time the United States sought permission to construct a canal, a precedent had already been set to use military force for defense of U.S. interests in Panama.[17]

The U.S. effort to build a canal required a concession from Colombia that would allow the United States to complete the bankrupt French project abandoned in 1889. In early 1903, the details were set down in a treaty ratified by the U.S. Senate, but unanimously rejected by the Colombian legislature. The United States responded by reaching out to the growing Panamanian secessionist movement. On November 3, 1903, in a quick and bloodless move encouraged by the offshore presence of U.S. warships, Panama separated from Colombia. The United States immediately recognized Panama as an independent state, and in return, Panama signed the Hay-Buneau-Varilla Treaty, ceding to the United States the rights to construct a canal and control it "in perpetuity."[18]

The Panama Canal opened in 1914, leading to U.S. dominance in the economic and, at times, political life of Panama. Although both countries benefitted from its operations, the relationship was far from equal, which along with the perpetual U.S. presence generated a nagging resentment, frequent protests, and periodic violence over the tangible loss of national sovereignty. This tension remained a dominant feature of U.S.-Panamanian relations until the canal was ceded back to Panama in 1977 under terms defined in the Panama Canal Treaties signed by Presidents Jimmy Carter and Omar Torrijos. Tensions flared again in 1989 when the U.S. military invaded Panama to arrest then-chief of state General Manual Noriega on narcotics trafficking charges and for threatening U.S. personnel and property. The incursion, nonetheless, proved to be a catalyst for the return of democracy. Panama's decision to promote trade liberalization soon followed.[19]

The Canal and U.S. Trade Policy

The canal solidified Panama as a maritime economy and its return to Panamanian control raised expectations of greater economic benefits from its ownership. The canal operations by themselves account for approximately 6% of Panama's GDP, with the largest and fastest-growing traffic volume generated along the U.S. East Coast-to-Asia trade route (especially U.S.-China). About one-third of all cargo passing through the canal has its origin or destination in the United States. The canal's total economic impact, however, is far greater, supporting income and jobs in various services industries including warehousing, ship registry and repair, salvage operations, insurance, banking, and tourism. The two major ports at either end of the canal have been privatized and modernized, and a portion of the canal was widened in 2001, and Panama has undertaken a difficult and expensive challenge to enhance the capacity of the entire canal to accommodate much larger post-Panama ships.[20] Panama held a national referendum on the $5.25 billion expansion on October 22, 2006. It passed by a wide margin and the expansion is underway.

With transfer of the canal and its operations to Panama, the country also inherited a substantial amount of land and physical assets. The conversion of these assets to private use has been a boon to the Panamanian economy, but not without considerable costs and investment, as well. Privatization efforts eased the transformation of former U.S. government facilities to productive Panamanian use, which has included refurbishing of the Panamanian railroad by Kansas City Southern Railways, transforming the former Albrook base into residential housing, and developing a small foreign processing zone in the former Ft. Davis.[21]

The Panama-Pacific Special Economic Area (PPSEA) is perhaps the most ambitious of these projects. This public-private partnership, established in law, aspires to convert the former Howard Air Force Base into a "world class business center," with an emphasis on the export sector. Existing assets include housing and office buildings, a hospital, transportation infrastructure, fiber optic cable network, an 8,500-foot runway, and four hangar facilities. The government offers businesses various fiscal incentives and a streamlined regulatory process. Firms are required to commit to state-of-the-art practices that include adopting internationally accepted environment and labor standards.[22] With the assistance of the International Finance Corporation (IFC) of the World Bank, Panama is relying on a large global financing package to cover the initial investment needs.

The project aims at developing various businesses including computer technology, cell phone manufacturing, international call centers (Dell already operates one on site), aeronautical industry support, and others that require a well-trained work force. The IFC supports this project not only for its prospects as a business venture, but because it is forward looking rather than relying on the "maquiladora" business model common in much of the region.[23.]

At the start of the 21st century, the canal and close ties with the United States are still defining features of Panama's economy, but in the past these traits have hindered Panama's participation in regional integration. Although part of the Central American Integration System, a broadly focused political arrangement, Panama has declined to join the Central American Common Market, relying instead on the canal and the large U.S. economy as its economic anchors. Panama has had a fully dollarized monetary system since independence and is a beneficiary of U.S. unilateral trade preferences defined in the Caribbean Basin Economic Recovery Act (CBERA), the Caribbean Basin Trade Partnership Act (CBTPA), and the Generalized System of Preferences (GSP).[24] These historical circumstances have given Panama little incentive to become a more open economy. Only since joining the World Trade Organization (WTO) in 1997 did Panama begin to reduce tariff rates, an important step in preparation for an FTA with the United States.

Panama's subregional independence and reliance on U.S. economic ties has suited the United States as well, given its continuing interest in the canal. An FTA with Panama may be seen as one way for the United States to support long-established commercial interests and deepen bilateral relations, particularly if accepted as a mutually beneficial pact with reasonably balanced political and economic outcomes. Although many ships have outgrown the canal, its locale and prospects for enlarging the passageway continue to reinforce Panama's historic, albeit currently diminished, importance for the United States as a strategic trade passage. A bilateral FTA with Panama also supported the Bush Administration's "competitive liberalization" trade strategy, in which negotiations were pursued simultaneously on multilateral, regional, and bilateral levels. This multi-tiered strategy is predicated on an expectation that gains on one level of negotiation may encourage, if not compel, breakthroughs on others. Because of slow progress on the WTO Doha Round and failure of the Free Trade Area of the Americas (FTAA), this strategy played out through aggressive bilateral trade negotiations, of which the Panama FTA is one. Some, however, have questioned the bilateral approach for the asymmetrical negotiation power the United States wields, the negative effects it may have on non-participating countries, and the one-sided trading system that could be developing around a U.S. hub, as opposed to a truly large regional or multilateral system. For Panama, the FTA reinforces its many trade policy goals and supports continued U.S. foreign direct investment. The services sector is already globally competitive, but the manufacturing sector is small and the agricultural sector remains protected and uncompetitive (see below). For Panama, the chief concern was crafting an

FTA that would balance the need to pursue openness for services, export growth and promotion for manufacturing, and adjustment time for agriculture to become more competitive, while minimizing social displacement. The incentive to negotiate was perhaps also enhanced by the desire to keep pace with other Latin American countries that already have or are negotiating FTAs with the United States.

PANAMANIAN TRADE RELATIONS

Panama is a country of 3.5 million people with a stable, diversified economy that has experienced strong growth despite the 2007-2008 global economic downturn. Panama's gross domestic product (GDP) expanded by an annual average of over 8% for the five years ending 2010. The economy grew by an robust 10.5% in 2011 (see Appendix B for selected macroeconomic data). Panama has the highest per capita income in the Central American region, but income distribution is highly skewed; poverty remains a nagging problem, especially in rural areas; and the unemployment rate has been moderately high. Inflation rose significantly in 2007-2008, but retreated in the following years. Unlike any other Latin American country, 77% of Panama's GDP is in services, developed around the transportation and commerce generated by canal traffic and the Colón Free Zone (CFZ). Industry is the second-most important sector, contributing 17% to GDP, followed by agriculture, contributing 6% to GDP.[25]

Structure and Direction of Panamanian Trade

Trade is an increasingly important part of this largely services-based economy, but as seen in Table 1, Panama has a historically large merchandise trade deficit, exporting relatively little compared to the amount of goods it imports.

From 2001 to 2011, Panama's annual merchandise trade deficits ranged from $696 million to $6.8 billion. Panama's declining terms of trade are one factor affecting the trade balance (see Appendix B), but the large increases beginning in 2007 reflect two developments. First, a large rise in oil imports driven by price and quantity, and an increase in construction machinery imports (derricks, dozers, cranes, etc.) related to Panama's strong economic growth, canal expansion, and other infrastructure investment.

Table 1. Panama's Merchandise and Services Trade Balances (U.S. $ millions)

	2001	2002	2003	2004	2005	2006	2007	2008	2009	2010	2011
Merchandise Trade Balance	-696	-1,035	-1,202	-1,537	-1,558	-1,712	-3,190	-4,546	-2,123	-4,616	-6,760
Services Trade Balance	890	968	1,240	1,337	1,420	2,273	2,836	3,155	3,328	3,333	3,349

Source: United Nations Economic Commission on Latin America and the Caribbean. *Preliminary Overview of the Economies of Latin America and the Caribbean,* December 2011, p. 100.

Panama tends to run a large services trade surplus, ranging from $890 million in 2001 to $3.4 billion in 2011. Such a large services component of the balance of payments is unusual for a Latin American country, but reflects the unique aspects of the Panamanian economy. In many years, the services surplus has balanced out most of the merchandise deficit. Since 2010, however, Panama has had much larger merchandise trade deficits, which may continue as long as energy and food prices remain high and the canal expansion accelerates.

Panama's trade policy emphasizes increased exports as a driver of economic growth, pointing to the Panama Pacific Special Economic Area, Colón Free Zone (see below), and to a lesser extent, the small export processing zones and nontraditional agricultural products as opportunities to execute this vision. Panama is a global trader and since 2002 has ratified FTAs with Canada, Chile, Costa Rica, Cuba, the Dominican Republic, El Salvador, Guatemala, Honduras, Nicaragua, Singapore, and Taiwan. It is also a party to an Association (limited) agreement between Central America and the European Union. Trade agreement negotiations are in process with Colombia, Peru, and the European Free Trade Association (EFTA) countries. Panama has also expressed interest in negotiating agreements with South Korea, the Caribbean Community (CARICOM) countries, and Gulf Cooperation Council.[26]

In 2011, the United States was Panama's largest export market, accounting for 20.8% of Panamanian exports, down sharply from 42.6% in 2009 (see Figure 2). Canada and Asia, by contrast, represent 15.4% and 14.7% of total Panamanian exports, respectively, growing significantly in recent years. This shift in export shares reflects a large decline in the value of fish exports to the United States and large increases in the value of commodity exports to Canada (gold), China (aluminum and copper), and Taiwan (iron and steel). The high prices of commodities, particularly gold, are a driving factor in the changed relative importance of Panama's export markets. The Latin American countries collectively are Panama's second-largest trading partner with a 21.1% share of Panama's exports.

The United States is also the largest import supplier to Panama, accounting for 24.9% of Panama's total imports, down from 29.1% in 2009. Latin America accounts for 20.7% of Panama's imports and Asia 13.4%. Panamanian trade has two distinct elements of importance on the import side. Nearly 12% of imports entered Panama through the Colon Free Zone (CFZ), discussed in detail below. In addition, another nearly 20% of imports reflect petroleum products entered through the Oil Import Zone (OIZ). Most of these imports originated in the United States, Latin America, and the Caribbean.

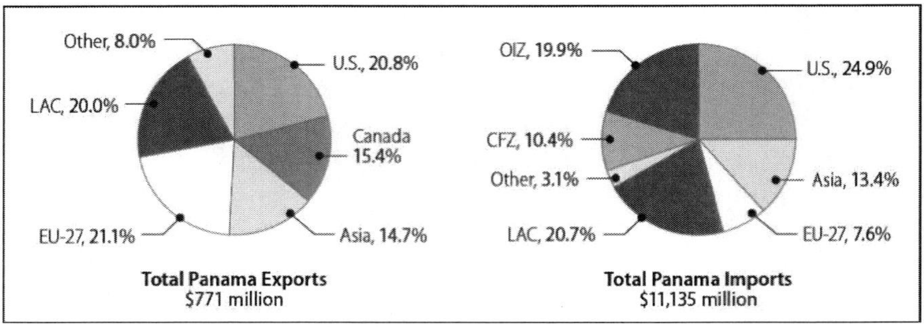

Source: CRS, from Global Trade Atlas data.

Figure 2. Panama Direction of Trade, 2011.

Panama is closely tied to the United States as its dominant trading partner, and is one of the few Latin American countries with which the United States has a merchandise trade surplus. Although small relative to total U.S. trade, it is by far the largest in the region. Panama runs a sizeable trade deficit with Latin America as well. Its largest Latin American trade partners are Costa Rica, Mexico, and Colombia. Panama also imports significant quantities of oil from Trinidad and Tobago. Trade with Asia follows the fast-paced commodity export pattern seen in many Latin American countries, with relatively modest growth in Panamanian imports from the region.

The Colón Free Zone

A distinct feature of Panama's trade regime is the Colón Free Zone (CFZ), which with the exception of Hong Kong is the largest duty free zone in the world. The vast trade volume that traverses the Panama Canal, multimodal transportation infrastructure, modern financial sector, and Panama's central location in the Americas make Colón a logical, if not ideal, place for a duty free zone. It serves as a "one stop shop" for both Latin American buyers and sellers from the rest of the world, including Asia and the United States. Sellers operate showrooms targeted at small-and medium-sized buyers, who make wholesale purchases of goods for retail sale in their respective countries. Goods are typically repackaged in smaller lots, priced in the local market currency, and transferred to the purchasing country without incurring income, value added, or transfer taxes. Most CFZ trade is in electronics, clothing, jewelry, and other luxury goods.

Buyers benefit from the ability to purchase in small lots, reduced travel costs, consolidated shipping, improved shipping times, and credit offered by sellers. The sellers benefit from reaching smaller Latin American markets in one location and reduced tax and transaction costs. Panama benefits from the 20,000 direct jobs the CFZ creates and the public revenue they generate. CFZ trade is reported as a separate component of Panama's trade statistics and only those goods entering the Panamanian economy are recorded as imports.[27]

The CFZ is frequently associated with a number of illicit activities including money laundering, illegal transshipment, and trademark and other intellectual property violations. In part, this is a reputation that Panama as a whole has been fighting since the military dictatorship, which was widely known for its flagrant disrespect of the law, if not outright corruption. Panama's proximity to Colombia and increased transshipment of illegal drugs in the region also fueled this perception.

The CFZ has attempted to counter this reputation. The zone itself is an enclosed commercial area, encircled by and under the supervision of customs and other law enforcement agencies of the Republic of Panama. In addition, both the Colón Free Zone User's Association and the CFZ Administration have a strict code of conduct and argue that illicit activity is also policed by individual companies because a bad reputation hurts those dedicated to making the CFZ a world class trading center. Even the accusation of an infraction can lead to a suspension of the license needed to operate in the zone. Cash accounts for only 10% of transactions and there is careful monitoring of all goods that move in and out of the zone through electronic tracking systems.[28]

U.S.-Panama Merchandise Trade

U.S.-Panamanian merchandise trade is small, as seen in Table 2.[29] In 2011, the United States exported $8,252.6 million worth of goods and imported $389.2 million, producing a U.S. trade surplus of $7,863.4 million, the largest in the Western Hemisphere. Still, Panama ranked as only the 32nd-largest export market for U.S. goods and 101st for imports. Major U.S. exports include oil and mostly capital- and technology-intensive manufactured goods such as aircraft, machinery, electrical machinery, pharmaceuticals, and motor vehicles.

The United States imports relatively little from Panama, accounting for the growing U.S. merchandise trade surplus. Most imports are primary products; 21% is seafood, mostly fresh fish and shrimp. Repaired goods account for one-third of total imports from Panama.[30] Commodity trade includes precious metals (mostly gold), fruit, sugar, and coffee, which together account for one-third of total U.S. imports. Unlike the Central American countries, where U.S. sensitivities to textile and apparel trade run high, Panama trades little in this sector. Panama's agricultural exports, particularly sugar, presented one of the more difficult negotiation challenges.

Table 2. U.S.-Panama Merchandise Trade, 2011
(top 10 U.S. exports and imports by $ value and as % of total)

U.S. Exports	$ Value million	% of Total	U.S. Imports	$ Value million	% of Total
1. Oil (not crude)	3,985.4	48.3	1. Repaired Goods	127.8	32.9
2. Machinery	624.4	7.6	Fish/Seafood	80.5	20.7
Aircraft	517.1	6.3	3. Gold	64.1	16.5
4. Electrical Machinery	477.8	5.8	4. Sugar	38.3	9.8
5. Repaired Goods	340.4	4.1	5. Edible Fruit	19.6	5.1
6. Vehicles	248.1	3.0	6. Coffee	8.2	2.1
7. Cereals	158.5	1.9	7. Aluminum	7.0	1.8
8. Organic Chemicals	152.1	1.8	8. Beverages	4.4	1.1
9. Perfume	144.8	1.8	9. Electrical Mach.	4.1	1.1
10. Pharmaceutical Goods	133.0	1.6	10. Copper	3.7	1.0
Other	1,471.0	17.8	Other	30.5	7.9
Total	8,252.6	100.0	Total	389.2	100.0

Source: U.S. Department of Commerce data presented by Global Trade Atlas.

U.S. Foreign Direct Investment

Panama has no formal restrictions on capital flows, does not discriminate between foreign and domestic investment, and maintains bilateral investment treaties with the United States and many European countries. Critics have pointed out, however, that the legal environment can be cumbersome and that Panama's relatively high labor costs (for the hemisphere) and inflexible labor laws can be a frustration if not an impediment to U.S. foreign direct investment (FDI).[31] Still, U.S. companies are well represented in Panama, including the largest container port facility in the region, multiple financial institutions, transportation firms, and manufacturing facilities from various sectors. Like other countries pursuing an FTA with the United States, Panama seeks closer ties for the continued FDI that may be generated from having a permanent rules-based trade relationship with a large trading partner.

U.S. FDI represents over a third of total FDI in Panama. Table 3 compares U.S. FDI in Panama to other regional destinations. The dollar value of U.S. investment in Panama is often nearly equal to that of the five Central American countries combined, and amounts to over 25% of Panama's GDP, compared to only 6% for Central America. The widening and expansion of the Panama Canal offers opportunity for some $5 billion of investment in the canal itself, and related large amounts of FDI for other sectors of the economy with a significant U.S. presence.

Table 3. U.S. Foreign Direct Investment in Panama, Mexico, and Central America ($ millions)

	2001	2002	2003	2004	2005	2006	2007	2008	2009	2010	2011
Panama	5,141	5,842	5,409	4,919	4,826	4,636	6,171	5,963	6,523	5,562	5,592
Mexico	52,544	56,303	56,851	63,384	73,687	82,965	91,046	87,443	82,286	84,288	91,402
Central America	2,994	3,199	2,333	4,834	3,902	4,031	5,217	7,840	6,523	6,399	6,618

Source: U.S. Department of Commerce. Bureau of Economic Analysis. BEA website accessed November 7, 2012. Data are stock of foreign direct investment (FDI) presented on a historical-cost basis.

SUMMARY OF TRADE NEGOTIATIONS AND THE U.S. PANAMA FTA

Panama approached the United States for a stand-alone FTA, preferring to avoid a direct link to the U.S.-Dominican Republic-Central America Free Trade Agreement (CAFTA-DR). Panama wanted to maximize an FTA's potential to win U.S. congressional approval by emphasizing the historical and strategic nature of the U.S.-Panamanian relationship, while separating the negotiations from the divisive CAFTA-DR accord. Panama's service economy, small textile and apparel industry, and limited integration with the Central American economies also bolstered the case for separate negotiations.[32] Another unique feature of the FTA negotiations was the treatment of business issues with respect to the Panama Canal Area. Its status as an autonomous legal entity under the Panamanian Constitution required separate negotiations for government procurement, labor, investment, and other areas.

The agreement was completed in 10 rounds of negotiation, concluding on December 16, 2006, and in general follows the text framework of earlier FTAs. It was signed on June 28, 2007, following some significant last minute changes to the labor, environment, intellectual property rights, and government procurement chapters to accommodate new commitments agreed to by the Bush Administration and bipartisan congressional leadership (the May 10th agreement). Market access schedules, drawn from previous FTA templates, reflect both U.S. and Panamanian interests, as do other market access provisions.

Congress requires that the United States International Trade Commission (USITC) make an economic assessment of the potential impact of an FTA on the U.S. economy. The analysis usually is done with both a general equilibrium model to estimate economy-wide changes and a partial equilibrium model to estimate sector or industry-level changes. In Panama's case, there were insufficient data to make a meaningful estimate from a general equilibrium model, and so detailed estimates of how the FTA might affect U.S. economic growth, employment, trade, and income were not offered. In general, however, through other quantitative and qualitative indicators, the USITC concluded that because Panama's economy is very small relative to that of the United States, the likely overall effect on the U.S. economy will be similarly very small.[33]

At the sector level, the USITC finds that the "main effect" of the FTA would likely be to increase U.S. exports, while causing little growth in U.S. imports from Panama. In general, the estimates are in line with general expectations based on (1) the small amount of goods imported from Panama; (2) the small production capacity of Panama; and (3) the fact that most imports from Panama (96% by value) already enter the United States duty free through either normal trade relations (NTR) or preferences provided by the Caribbean Basin Initiative (CBI) programs or the Generalized System of Preferences (GSP).[34]

Detailed estimates suggest that when fully implemented, the largest growth potentially will accrue to U.S. exports of rice (145%), pork (96%), beef (94%), and passenger vehicles (43%). Again, these would amount to a very small dollar value increase given that, with the exception of rice, the U.S. exports of these goods to Panama represent less than two-tenths of one percent (0.2%) of U.S. exports to the world and even a smaller portion of U.S. production. With respect to the services provisions in the FTA, they exceed

WTO commitments, but the gains for U.S. providers are also expected to be small, with the potential for further gains once the Panama Canal expansion project is fully underway.[35]

Below is a more detailed discussion of the major negotiation areas and an analysis of the issues that have been of particular interest to Panama and the United States, including the U.S. Congress. Where relevant, changes made pursuant to the May 10 bipartisan agreement are highlighted.

Market Access

Market access (chapter 3 of the FTA) covers provisions that govern barriers to trade such as tariffs, quotas, safeguards, other nontariff barriers, and rules of origin (chapter 4). The U.S.- Panama FTA replaces duty-free treatment extended selectively by unilateral trade preferences provided to Panama under the Caribbean Basin Economic Recovery Act (CBERA), the Caribbean Basin Trade Partnership Act (CBTPA), and the Generalized System of Preferences (GSP), under which some Panamanian goods enter the United States duty free.[36] Most goods entering into the United States duty free do so under normal trade relations (NTR).

Panamanian agricultural products, however, do face some of the highest barriers, particularly sugar, which is subject to a tariff rate quota (TRQ). Panama levies an average tariff of 7% on U.S. industrial and consumer goods, with tariff peaks of 81% for some goods. The average tariff on U.S. agricultural goods is 15%, with peaks as high as 260% on one product.[37] Imports also face an additional 5% transfer tax, which applies to domestic goods as well.

Market access provides for national treatment for traded goods of both parties, with a detailed schedule defining the progressive elimination of customs duties for manufactured and agricultural goods. There are nine staging categories that classify each country's goods based on the time to tariff elimination, with the most sensitive products given lengthier phase-out of tariffs. Tariffs on 88% of industrial and commercial goods go to zero immediately, with the remaining tariffs phased out over a 10-year period. Similarly, up to two-thirds of U.S. farm exports receive immediate duty free treatment.[38] Tariffs on some agricultural goods remain in place longer, with some taking up to 17 years to be completely eliminated (20 years for rice). Safeguards have been retained for many products only for the period of duty phase-out, but antidumping and countervailing duties were not addressed, leaving these trade remedy laws fully operational, as required under TPA negotiating objectives.

Rules of origin define which goods would be eligible for duty-free treatment based on the country of origin of their content. Rules of origin are intended to prevent transshipment of goods made from materials originating in countries outside the agreement. They are particularly pertinent to apparel and textile trade, of which there is very little exported from Panama.

Agricultural Trade

The United States has a small, but positive agricultural trade balance with Panama. Agriculture accounts for a small portion of total U.S. merchandise exports to Panama, but the United States captures some 51% of the Panamanian agricultural import market. While the average tariff on U.S. agricultural products is 15%, tariffs can peak as high as 260% for chicken leg quarters.[39] Because both countries had products they wished to protect, agriculture market access was one of the most difficult issues to resolve.

U.S. domestic agricultural support programs are not addressed in the FTA, which focuses on tariff reduction, quota definitions, and sanitary and phytosanitary (SPS) rules and enforcement measures. Market access was particularly difficult for four highly protected products: pork, poultry, rice, and sugar. The United States was basically “offensive” on pork, poultry, and rice, expecting to open Panama’s markets further. It was “defensive” on sugar, attempting to limit increases in the sugar quota that might disrupt operations of the U.S. sugar program as defined in legislation. Panama’s position was the reverse, pressing to minimize increases in U.S. exports of pork, poultry, and rice, and to increase its sugar export quota.

The U.S. sugar program reflects a historical commitment to protect the income of sugar beet, sugar cane, and sugar processing firms with below-prime-rate loans, limitations on sales in the domestic market, and tariff rate quotas (TRQs). TRQs restrict imports with prohibitively high tariffs on imports above a defined quota amount, as permitted under WTO rules. In FY2008, the above-quota tariff rate was estimated to be 86% on raw cane sugar and 76% on refined sugar.[40] For comparative purposes, on average, Panama harvests only a quarter of the sugar produced by each of the five Central American countries, but it still plays a disproportionally important role in the Panamanian agricultural sector. Sugar constitutes a third of Panama’s total agricultural exports, compared to less than 10% for the Central American countries, and 41% of agricultural exports to the United States. The U.S.

market consumes 76% of Panamanian sugar exports, compared to less than 10% of sugar exports from Central America.

Given the dependence of Panamanian sugar producers on the U.S. market, in part driven by the industry's relatively high wage rates that make it cost prohibitive to produce for the world market, the Panamanians argued that even a relatively small quantitative increase in their portion of the U.S. sugar quota would have a large benefit for their industry. The U.S. sugar industry, however, continued to resist the inclusion of sugar in bilateral FTAs, arguing that the WTO is the forum for addressing domestic support programs and TRQs in the agricultural sector.

For Panama, pork, rice, and poultry were the most sensitive products. These are also protected by TRQs, with in-quota tariffs of 15% and out-of-quota tariffs rising to 74%, 103%, and 273%, respectively. Pork and poultry have a special issue related to the consumption of white versus dark meat. The United States consumes considerably more white meat than dark, leaving a disproportional amount of dark cuts for export, which face the highest tariffs. In Panama, as with much of the world, dark meat is preferred. The concern revolved around U.S. producers' willingness to sell dark meat cuts at a low price in foreign markets, putting downward pressure on prices and hurting domestic producers in those countries. The Panamanians argued that because of the relatively high profit margins on white meat in the United States, on a cost allocation basis, U.S. producers can actually afford to sell the dark meat at below cost. The cost accounting can be debated, but concerns over the price effect in the Panamanian market remained unchanged.

Panama's rice industry, which supplies over 90% of the domestic demand, also argued that opening the market to U.S. subsidized rice would decimate their industry, which, because of its protection, sells rice considerably above the world price. In fact, the USITC report estimates that when fully implemented, the FTA will have the greatest impact on U.S. rice exports. Although the rice provisions will not be fully implemented until year 20 of the agreement, for milled rice, the TRQ for the first year will be 20 times the current level of U.S. exports to Panama, which may be expected to affect rice growers shortly after implementation, perhaps causing them to shift production to other crops, or leave farming for alternative employment.[41]

Panamanian agriculture represents only 6% of GDP, but 17% of employment. These numbers point to both an inherent inefficiency, due in part to protection, but also the strong role agriculture plays in supporting rural employment and social stability. Agriculture's 17% of national employment actually supports 40% of the country's population living in rural areas, most of whom exist at or below the poverty line. Given the potential to dislocate much of the poor in the country, the Panamanians argued that opening the agricultural sector too quickly to the large production capacity of the United States would have been highly detrimental to the social structure of the rural economy, leading to increased unemployment, poverty, and rural-urban migration. For these reasons, Panama wanted a slow transition to open markets in the agriculture sector, as well as an increase in the sugar quota to boost employment. This would also buy time for Panama to develop its non-traditional export crops, such as melons, palm oil, and pineapples, which some view as the future of this sector.

The compromise struck in the FTA provides duty-free treatment for over half of U.S. farm exports to Panama including high quality beef, poultry products, soybeans, most fresh fruits, and a number of processed goods. Remaining tariffs will be phased out between years 7 and 17 of the FTA. Rice tariffs, which protect one of Panama's most sensitive products, will remain in place until year 20 of the FTA. U.S. exports of rice and other products receive expanded quotas under the Panamanian tariff rate quota system. The United States agreed to give Panama an additional 7,000 metric tons of sugar imports in the first year under a three-tiered TRQ system, which will grow by 1% per year, capped eventually for some types of sugar.[42]

Other protective measures for agriculture were negotiated. Whereas export subsidies, voluntary restrain agreements, and import licensing are generally prohibited, the FTA allows for TRQs, safeguards, and a sugar compensation mechanism. The sugar mechanism gives the United States the option to compensate Panamanian sugar producers in lieu of giving their exports duty-free treatment. This option could be employed if the U.S. sugar program were threatened with disruption.

Sanitary and Phytosanitary Standards (SPS)

SPS was one of the most difficult issues to resolve. Although understood as necessary to ensure the safety of agricultural imports, SPS standards can be a burden, and are often denounced as a veiled form of protectionism. Panama's SPS standards, on the whole, are considered to be very high and meet or exceed WTO standards. The USTR, however, has long raised concerns over procedural transparency with respect to phytosanitary permits and also Panama's requirement that imports of poultry, beef, and pork, its most protected products, come from processing plants that have been individually inspected by Panamanian officials. The United States contended that this process has often been cumbersome, drawn out, and ultimately very costly to U.S. producers.[43]

The United States wanted Panama to recognize the USDA certification process as equivalent to Panamanian standards for the purpose of securing unimpeded entry of U.S. meat exports. This issue became highly controversial during the ninth round of negotiations, when U.S. negotiators proposed this agreement be put into a formal side letter. Panama responded by noting that the SPS chapter had already been closed, that its meat inspection standards are among the highest in the world, and that a last minute effort to change SPS provisions raised sovereignty issues in Panama by potentially requiring Panama to lower its standards in some cases.[44]

As part of the resolution, Panamanian officials visited the United States to review the food safety inspection system for meat and poultry, and found that accepting the U.S. system would pose no sanitary threat to Panama. This understanding was formalized in a separate bilateral agreement between the two countries, along with a streamlined import documentation system. Signed and entered into force on December 20, 2006, the agreement states that for meat, poultry, dairy, and other processed products, Panama agrees to accept U.S. sanitary, phytosanitary, and regulatory systems as equivalent to those of Panama, and will no longer require individual plant inspections. Panama has since amended its laws accordingly.[45]

Textiles and Apparel

In general, textiles and apparel make for difficult market access negotiations, but Panama produces very little of these goods. The FTA would provide immediate duty-free access for all textile and apparel goods, subject to rules of origin (requiring use of fabric and yarn produced in Panama or the United States).[46] The permanence of the provisions and more accommodating measures provide a benefit to the small Panamanian industry. Safeguard measures would allow duties to increase on imports in which a sudden increase in volume either threatens or actually harms U.S. producers. The text also provides for short supply lists of fabrics, yarns, and fibers that otherwise would face duties. The market access provisions were not the major apparel issue. Because Panama is a huge transshipment point for international trade and has its own duty free zone, the main concern was to assure U.S. apparel producers that there would be effective customs cooperation to deter illegal transshipment of goods that do not meet rules of origin. There is an extensive provision on consultation, monitoring, and onsite visit procedures in support of adhering to the rules of origin.[47]

Government Procurement

Transparency in the bidding process for government contracts was listed as one of the most important issues by the U.S. Chamber of Commerce in Panama.[48] Some of the concerns expressed were addressed in the 2006 amendments to the procurement law, which codified advancements such as allowing use of Internet procurement. These changes modernized and made more transparent procurement regulations, government purchasing information, and transactions. A separate administrative court for public contracting disputes was also created. These changes enhanced Panamanian laws that already require transparency in the bidding process. Panama has not acceded to the WTO Government Procurement Agreement, which the United States has encouraged.[49]

The government procurement chapter differs from earlier FTAs by stating that a firm's adherence to "acceptable" environmental and labor standards may be included as a standard in the bidding and procurement process. The technical specifications article states that it is not intended to preclude a procuring entity from using technical specifications to promote conservation of natural resources, or to require a supplier to comply with generally applicable laws regarding fundamental principles and rights to work; and acceptable conditions of work with respect to minimum wages, hours of work, and occupation safety and health in the territory in which the good is produced or the service is performed.

Government procurement takes on a greater importance when considered in light of the Panama Canal expansion and related prospects for large long-term investments. The Panama Canal Authority (PCA) operates independently of the national government, and Panama required separate negotiation apart from the regular government procurement chapter.

Panama negotiated to maintain the canal authority dispute settlement system within the FTA, as well as to keep small business set aside provisions for Panamanian firms. In addition, for 12 years after the agreement takes effect, Panama may set aside contracts let by the PCA to Panamanian firms subject to clear notice of intent to do so and limitations on the size of contracts.

The text otherwise addresses U.S. concerns over nondiscriminatory, fair, and open government procurement procedures for all national government authorities. Like the PCA, subnational governments (e.g., states and municipalities) are not required to uphold the government procurement provisions, but those willing to do so appear in an appendix of the FTA.

Investment

Panama has a well-developed financial services industry to support the flow of capital and is an important regional financial center. U.S. firms invest heavily in Panama relative to other Latin American countries, and a permanent rules-based trade agreement may be seen as enhancing this relationship. Panama signed a bilateral investment treaty with the United States in 1991, the first in the region, which includes investor-state provisions and further guarantees of the free flow of transfers under a 1998 law. Although the Panamanian government has been responsive to U.S. foreign investment interests, concerns have arisen in particular cases involving investment in highly regulated industries. Resolution of these concerns facilitated the FTA negotiations and the potential exists for further significant foreign investment in Panama, including the canal expansion and reverted areas of the former canal zone.[50]

The FTA text provides for clear and enforceable rules for foreign investments, which is largely accomplished by "standard" language requiring national and most-favored-nation (nondiscriminatory) treatment. It further clarifies rules on expropriation (including indirect expropriation) and compensation, investor-state dispute settlement, and the expeditious free flow of payments and transfers related to investments, with certain exceptions in cases subject to legal proceedings (e.g., bankruptcy, insolvency, criminal activity). Transparent and impartial dispute settlement procedures provide recourse to investors.

Two investment issues stand out. First is the investor-state provision, which was controversial during the CAFTA-DR debate, but is commonly used in U.S. bilateral investment treaties (BITs) and in earlier FTAs. It allows investors alleging a breach in investment obligations to seek binding arbitration against the state through the dispute settlement mechanism defined in the Investment Chapter. U.S. investors have long supported the inclusion of investor-state rules to ensure that they have recourse in countries that may lack the institutional capacity to adequately protect the legal rights of foreign investors. Since bilateral investment treaties usually have been made with developing countries that have little foreign investment in the United States, it was not anticipated that these provisions would be applied in the United States. Circumstances changed under NAFTA, when investor-state provisions gave rise to "indirect expropriation" claims against subnational (state) governments in the United States over environmental and other regulations.[51]

Although none of the claimants filing against the United States has prevailed, Congress instructed in Trade Promotion Authority (TPA) legislation that future trade agreements ensure "that foreign investors in the United States are not accorded greater substantive rights with respect to investment protections than United States investors." In response, Annex 10-B of the U.S.- Panama FTA states that "except in rare circumstances, nondiscriminatory regulatory actions by a Party that are designed and applied to protect legitimate welfare objectives, such as public health, safety, and the environment, do not constitute indirect expropriations." This provision, along with one that allows for early elimination of "frivolous" suits, is intended to address these concerns, although some stakeholders remain skeptical.[52]

Second, Annex 10-F of the FTA seeks to reserve certain rights with respect to disputes filed under Section - B of the investment chapter that may affect the Panama Canal Authority (PCA). First, Annex 10-F clarifies that Panama has sole authority over the canal and its operations, and should a claim be made against the PCA, the dispute tribunal "may not order attachment or enjoin the application of a measure that has been adopted or maintained by the Panama Canal Authority in pursuance of" its responsibility for the canal. Second, a claim arising from acts of the PCA that alleges a breach of the investment agreement must first be made to the PCA, where it will have three months to respond before the claim may be made to the dispute settlement panel under the FTA.

Services

Services trade was negotiated in multiple chapters and includes financial services, shipping, telecommunications, professional services, and e-commerce. Panama is a service-based economy, has many competitive services industries, and is known for its "open regulatory environment for services." In general, the FTA provides for market access commitments in services that exceeds the WTO General Agreement on Trade in Services (GATS). With the possible exception of future canal expansion projects, the USITC estimates that the new commitments, although important changes, will have only a small economic impact on U.S. providers.[53]

Panama requires local licensing for many professionals to practice in the country, which the United States wanted to change, but was only partially successful in some cases (e.g., lawyers). Panama was the first country in Latin America to pass e-commerce legislation. It recognizes the legal standing of electronic transactions and provides for the creation of an oversight agency. The United States pressed for even greater transparency in regulatory procedures and U.S. business groups identified services as a critical negotiating area given U.S. competitive advantages and the large services sector in Panama.[54]

Equal ability to compete in retail trade, express delivery, and financial services, including insurance and portfolio management, was achieved in the FTA, an issue of primary importance to the United States. In particular, restrictions on investment in retail trade and access to contracts let by the Panama Canal Authority were either eliminated or reduced. Greater access to other professional services and transparency in licensing and other accreditation were clarified. To the extent that restrictions in these areas are reduced, U.S. firms are better able to compete in the largest sector of the Panamanian economy, the one most likely to grow with canal expansion and increased merchandise trade through the canal. Panama wanted greater transparency in the U.S. state-level financial services regulatory system to help ease the possible opening of Panamanian banks in select U.S. states. The United States government argued, however, that it was unable to make commitments on state-level financial services regulatory matters.

Intellectual Property Rights

Strengthening intellectual property rights (IPR) was a major U.S. priority, in particular by harmonizing standards at U.S. levels, and by securing Panama's commitment to join an array of international agreements related to IPR protection. The most contentious IPR issues revolved around patent and data exclusivity issues related to pharmaceutical products, but Internet piracy also became a serious problem.

The USTR reports that Panama's IPR laws and institutional support have improved with the creation of courts dedicated specifically to IPR cases. Panama updated its patent law in 1996 and has a law governing trademark protection. Panama signed on to the World Intellectual Property Organization (WIPO) Copyright Treaty and Performances and Phonographs Treaty. The 1994 copyright law improved protection and increased the options to prosecute violators. The United States continues to encourage Panama to accede to additional IPR treaties, as now required in the FTA, and to remain vigilant in its antipiracy commitment, a primary concern given the large amount of goods that are shipped through the Canal Free Zone.[55]

IPR provisions in the FTA exceed those in the WTO. They provide that all businesses receive equal treatment and that Panama ratify or accede to various international IP agreements. Trademark registration is better enforced through a transparent online process and special system to resolve disputes over Internet domain issues, among other requirements. Copyright provisions clarify use of digital materials (exceeding TRIPS standards) including rights over temporary copies of works on computers (music, videos, software, text), sole author rights for making their work available online, extended terms of protection for copyrighted materials, strong anti-circumvention provisions to prohibit tampering with technologies, the requirement that governments use only legitimate computer software, the prohibition of unauthorized receipt or distribution of encrypted satellite signals, and rules for liability of Internet service providers for copyright infringement. Patents and trade secrets rules conform more closely with U.S. norms. End-user piracy is criminalized and all parties are required to authorize the seizure, forfeiture, and destruction of counterfeit and pirated goods. The text also mandates statutory damages for abuse of copyrighted material.[56]

Pharmaceutical Issues

The U.S.-Panama FTA adopts new IPR pharmaceutical standards that reflect a bipartisan understanding as developed by congressional leadership and the USTR in the May 10, 2007, agreement. They affect three important issues. The first and perhaps most complicated issue is *data exclusivity*. To bring a patented drug to market, a drug company must demonstrate through clinical trials that the drug is both safe and effective, a time-consuming and costly process. Under U.S. law, the data used to establish these claims are protected for a period of five years from the time the patented drug is approved for use in a country's market, the so-called data exclusivity term. Under this protection, regulatory agencies cannot use these data or rely on references to such data in the certification of a generic version of the medicine or drug until the data exclusivity period ends. This issue was raised by Members of Congress and others during the CAFTA-DR debate, but was only partially addressed in a side agreement ("understanding") assuring that relevant WTO rules would be in force. Critics, however, wanted the side agreement to include an explicit exception to the data protection requirement for cases where compulsory licensing under the WTO rules might be invoked, and to include the language in the body of the FTA.[57]

Congressional input led to significant changes to the Panama text. The IPR chapter provides that if a company files to bring to market a new drug in a foreign country (e.g., Panama), and the foreign regulatory agency relies on marketing approval of the initial filing in the home country (e.g., the United States) for approval in Panama, and the Panamanian regulatory agency approves the drug within six months of that filing, the data exclusivity term begins at the time the drug was approved in the United States, not Panama. This provision is intended to speed the entry of generic drugs into Panama's market by encouraging both drug companies and foreign governments to engage in the approval process as quickly and efficiently as possible. Because the six-month rule effectively reduces the data exclusivity term in Panama, drug companies are encouraged to file as soon as feasible to maximize the time their data may be protected in Panama after receiving market approval. Because countries must approve within the sixth-month rule to benefit from it, they are encouraged to put in place an efficient drug certification process.[58]

In addition, there is language in the IPR chapter stating that in cases such as epidemics, extreme urgency or national emergency, and other cases of public non-commercial use, a waiver from the data exclusivity laws would be allowed. The WTO public health provisions allow for compulsory licensing, circumventing patents in public health emergencies or other circumstances of public use deemed necessary. In the case of the U.S.-Panama FTA, which requires a period of data exclusivity not mandated by the WTO, the waiver is extended to the data exclusivity term as well.

A second issue is *patent term restoration*, which allows for the retroactive application of patents in cases where the approval process for a patent extends beyond some legal- or regulatory-determined standard period of time. Although there are provisions that require term restoration for patents in general, in the case of pharmaceutical products, term extension is only optional.

The third issue is *patent linkage*. This term refers to linking the sanitary registration process (done, for example, by the Food and Drug Administration in the United States) with the patent registration process. U.S. firms effectively wanted mandatory linkage that would automatically check for patent infringement when an application for bringing a drug to market is made in a foreign country sanitary registration office. The Panama agreement was amended to make patent linkage voluntary, and allows for administrative or judicial remedies to expedite patent challenges.

Public health advocates have long pushed for re-balancing international rules in ways that would facilitate the introduction of lower-cost generic equivalents into developing countries. The revised IPR chapter in the Panama FTA supports congressional interest in pursuing this goal, although not to the full satisfaction of some public health advocates. Drug originating pharmaceutical companies, by contrast, lobbied against these changes, arguing that they bear their full cost through cumbersome administration and lost revenue by the earlier introduction of generic competition. They further argued that they count on this revenue to offset the high costs of research and development that allow new drugs to be properly tested and approved in the first place.

Labor and Environment

Labor and environmental provisions have been highly contentious issues in trade agreements, with considerable disagreement in Congress and elsewhere over how aggressive language in trade agreements should be in accommodating these concerns. An important aspect of the U.S.-Panama FTA is that it adopts new standards for both the labor and environment chapters that reflect a 2007 bipartisan understanding as developed by congressional leadership and the USTR. Despite the bipartisan nature of the agreement, some Members continue to express reservations about the effectiveness of labor provisions, as well as the overall benefits of bilateral FTAs.

The debate over labor and environmental standards reflects differences in both economic and political perspectives. From an economic perspective, it has been argued that developing country firms may have an "unfair" competitive advantage because their lower standards are a basis for their lower costs, which in turn are reflected in lower prices for goods that may compete with those produced in developed countries.[59]

It follows from this argument that the difference in costs may be an inducement to move U.S. investment and jobs abroad. In addition, critics have also argued that trade agreements should not support production standards that lead to unacceptable working conditions or severe environmental degradation.

On the other hand, some studies have suggested that cost differentials are usually not high enough to determine business location alone, and that productivity is the more important factor.[60] Further, many economists view trade liberalization as part of the overall development process that, in and of itself, can promote improved social and economic conditions over the long run.[61] Developing countries are also concerned with the possible loss of sovereignty should specific standards be defined in trade agreements, as well as with the possibility that such provisions can be misused as a disguised form of protectionism.

Labor Issues

Preliminary drafts of the U.S.-Panama FTA adopted the CAFTA-DR labor chapter language verbatim. Many Members of Congress and others objected to four key aspects of this language. First, it emphasized that a country must effectively "enforce its own labor laws," rather than define specific labor standards to be codified and enforced.[62] Second, this was the only provision in the labor chapter subject to the FTA's labor dispute resolution process (other commitments were unenforceable). Third, labor (and environment) provisions had their own dispute settlement mechanism separate from the process used for commercial and other disputes. Critics charged that the labor dispute mechanism was inferior for many reasons. Fourth, language that required Parties to the agreement only to "strive to ensure" that they do not waive or derogate from their labor law commitments was considered both inadequate and unenforceable.

In short, there existed a basic criticism that the labor provisions in the bilateral FTAs did not reflect the intent of Congress in defining labor negotiating objectives in Trade Promotion Authority (TPA) legislation, were a step backward in U.S. policy on this issue that conditions trade benefits on meeting basic ILO labor commitments as defined in the Caribbean Basin Initiative (CBI) and the Generalized System of Preferences (GSP), and were effectively meaningless without a credible enforcement mechanism.[63]

Although supporters of the CAFTA-DR model prevailed in earlier agreements, a new bipartisan consensus emerged with the 110th congressional leadership that led to a significantly changed model for bilateral FTA labor chapters. The principles of this change, as defined in the May 10, 2007, agreement, were incorporated into the labor chapters for U.S. bilateral FTAs with Panama, Peru, Colombia, and South Korea. The major changes from the CAFTA-DR model state that each country

- shall adopt and maintain in its statutes, regulations and practices as rights, the five core ILO labor principles: freedom of association; the effective recognition of the right to collective bargaining; the elimination of all forms of compulsory or forced labor; the effective abolition of child labor and, for purposes of this Agreement, a prohibition on the worst forms of child labor; and, the elimination of discrimination in respect of employment and occupation;
- shall not waive or otherwise derogate from, or offer to do so, in a manner affecting trade or investment between the countries in implementing the above commitment;

- shall not fail to effectively enforce its labor laws in accordance with the above commitment and that each party retains the right to the reasonable exercise of discretion in using resources to achieve this goal, provided the exercise of such discretion is not inconsistent with the obligations of the chapter, and;
- will be required to use the dispute settlement process defined for the entire agreement (rather than a separate process for labor disputes as defined in the CAFTA-DR).

The change in language is intended to make commitments to ILO basic principles binding and enforceable to the same extent as all other commitments in the FTA, including having recourse to trade sanctions. The rest of the labor chapter conforms largely to commitments in previous bilateral FTAs. These include procedural guarantees of transparency and fairness in the use of tribunals to enforce a Party's labor laws and institutional arrangements that include creation of a joint Labor Affairs Council to oversee implementation and review of commitments made in the Labor Chapter. A new Labor Cooperation and Capacity Building Mechanism is also to be established.

Panama's Labor Code and Conditions

Panama has higher wage rates, stronger labor laws, and fewer impediments to union formation than many countries in the region. The business community, including U.S. firms operating in Panama, argues that the labor laws are too generous with respect to firing or downsizing the labor force, which can actually encourage unintended responses by business, such as extended use of temporary workers. In 1970, Panama created the Tripartite Council on Union Freedom and Participation in Economic and Social Development with representatives from the government, labor, and business. Its primary function is to oversee that workers' rights are being observed in Panama. The U.S. State Department notes that Panama's labor laws guarantee all the ILO basic principles. All private-sector and most public-sector employees have the right to organize, bargain collectively, and strike (limited for the public sector). In general, major violations of labor laws have not been found, but the ILO has raised concerns about a number of ongoing practices. These include the widespread use of temporary workers to circumvent the labor code, the minimum requirement of 40 workers to form a union, and the use of child labor, particularly in agricultural areas during harvest times and for domestic employment. Lax enforcement of health and safety standards was also cited as a continuing problem.[64] Some of these issues were cited by Members of Congress as needing to be addressed before the FTA could be considered (see "U.S. Congressional Action").[65]

Environmental Issues

Environmental specialists have stressed the need to achieve multiple goals in U.S. reciprocal FTAs. These include protecting and assuring strong enforcement of existing domestic environmental standards, ensuring that multilateral environmental agreements are not undermined by trade rules, promoting strong environmental initiatives to evaluate and raise performance, developing a systematic program of capacity-building assistance, and assuring that environmental provisions in FTAs are subject to the same dispute resolution and enforcement mechanisms as are other aspects of the agreements.[66] At issue is identifying and attempting to ameliorate the environmental effects of trade, particularly in developing countries that may have weak laws and lax enforcement mechanisms. Even among environmental experts, opinions vary. Some have suggested that thus far trade agreements have not led to catastrophic pollution nor encouraged a "regulatory race to the bottom." There has also been a certain acknowledged degree of success in having environmental issues addressed in the body of FTAs, in side agreements on environmental cooperation, and through technical assistance programs, which developing countries can use to respond to specific problems. Advocates and many Members of Congress still note that much can be improved, such as clarifying obligations, tightening enforcement language, and ensuring that the United States allocates financial resources to back up promises of technical assistance.[67] As with the FTA labor chapter, revisions made pursuant to ideas outlined in the arrangement of May 10, 2007, reflect a bipartisan sense of that although the text recognizes sovereign rights and responsibilities with respect to the management of natural resources, that trade and environmental policies should be mutually supportive and dedicated to the objective of sustainable development. The new language, therefore, strengthens the commitments to environmental obligations and their enforcement, requiring that each country

- adopt, maintain, and implement laws, regulations, and other measures to fulfill their obligations under selected multilateral environmental agreements (MEAs) listed in Annex 18.2;
- shall not fail to effectively enforce environmental laws and regulations, including those adopted as signatories to the MEAs;

- shall not waive or otherwise derogate from, or offer thereto, from such laws (replacing the "strive to ensure" language with "shall not");
- adopt a commitment to policies that will promote conservation and sustainable use of biological diversity;
- subject disputes to the FTA's overall dispute settlement mechanism rather than a mechanism developed solely to deal with labor and environmental disagreements that was used in previous FTAs, and;
- meet obligations for formal cooperation among governments on environmental issues and use of the consultation and dispute resolution mechanism in a way that is transparent and involves public input.[68]

As required under TPA, the USTR conducted an environmental review of the potential environmental effects possibly attributable to the FTA. It noted that Panama "faces a number of challenges in protecting its environment as it supports its economic and population growth." Deforestation, land degradation, loss of wildlife, and threats to water quality and wetlands, among other problems, are serious issues for Panama. The Panama Canal also places severe water use requirements on the country. Panama has responded through the public policy process, establishing environmental standards in law and entering into international and U.S. bilateral environmental cooperation agreements.[69] These issues were already factors in Panama's development process prior to the negotiation of the FTA. Thus, the environmental review maintains that the marginal effects of the FTA on environmental standards would be small, whether in terms of projected impacts on the United States or on Panama. The environmental review further notes that Panama's service-oriented economy and the small trade volume with the United States are unlikely to be greatly affected by the FTA and so will change production and trade little. Still, the FTA may have both positive and negative effects. The negative effects of pollution, environmental degradation, and endangering wildlife would come mostly from increased agricultural trade and production, which might be addressed with increased environmental oversight and policies. The positive effect of the FTA could include improvements in environmental standards that may be encouraged by the provisions of the agreement and the consultative and cooperation agreements attached to the FTA.[70] Panama's environmental regulatory agency points out that Panama is increasingly using environmental impact studies, but realizes it has enforcement capacity issues that may require time to remedy, which could be accommodated in the FTA.

Trade Capacity Building

The FTA would create a Committee on Trade Capacity Building (TCB) designed to assist Panama with the transition to freer trade with the United States. In general, the committee's mission includes providing technical assistance and coordinating financing to accelerate the transition period in expectation of increasing the gains of trade while minimizing the adjustment costs. The TCB Committee would help coordinate technical assistance provided by U.S., regional, and multilateral agencies in helping Panama meet its obligations under the FTA. Panama prioritized TCB needs in its national trade capacity building strategy. The overriding goal is to formulate a strategy that would allow Panama to assume all the commitments under the FTA, in the context of also meeting the country's development needs. The National TCB Strategy places strong emphasis on sectoral adjustment strategies, recognizing that some industries are already competitive by international standards (e.g., financial services), whereas others will need considerable assistance when faced with increased competition from the United States (e.g., agriculture). Emphasis is also placed on supporting existing and potentially new micro, small, and medium-sized businesses, which may need the most assistance and constitute a significant portion of the Panamanian economy, as well as government capacity to administer trade-related activities.[71]

The major goals identified include inter-sectoral coordination, increasing exports to the United States, enhancing the investment climate, better integrating education and innovation into the business community, and improving government trade facilitation (processing imports and exports). The strategy identifies 18 action plans covering major trade and trade-related issues, ranging from market access and rules of origin, to labor, environment, transparency, and trade agreement administration. In each case, the status of Panama's commitments under the FTA is identified along with action items that may need to be pursued to improve capacity in the respective area.

Successful implementation of the strategy, however, requires financial and technical resources coordinated among international and U.S. aid agencies. Already in place is a U.S. Agency for International Development (USAID) project to support Panama's transition to more open trade. It has two major initiatives: supporting implementation of the FTA and assisting Panama with sectoral adjustment to the increased competitiveness arising from international trade. In the first case, the USAID project has helped prepare and disseminate a product that explains the benefits of the FTA and how Panama might better access the U.S. market with its specific products.

The second initiative focuses on helping three major sectors of the economy, each with a differing level of product complexity, to increase their exposure and market share in the United States. Specifically, agro-industry, information and communications technology, and artisan products were identified as sectors with potential to benefit from the FTA. Sector strategies range from targeted product design, to "hands on" assistance in participating in trade fairs, and building contacts and linkages with venture capitalists and other key business facilitation professionals.[72]

APPENDIX A. CHRONOLOGY OF U.S.-PANAMA FTA MILESTONES

Date	Milestone
November 18, 2003	The USTR notifies Congress of President George W. Bush's intent to enter into negotiations on a free trade agreement (FTA) with the Republic of Panama.
April 26-29, 2004	First round of negotiations occurs in Panama City.
June 11-15, 2004	Second round of negotiations takes place in Los Angeles.
July 12-16, 2004	Third round of negotiations held in Panama City.
August 9-12, 2004	Fourth round of negotiations held in Tampa.
October 18-22, 2004	Fifth round of negotiations takes place in Panama City.
December 6-10, 2004	Sixth round of negotiations held in Washington, DC.
January 10-15, 2005	Seventh round of negotiations held in Washington, DC.
Jan. 31-Feb. 6, 2005	Eighth round of negotiations occurs in Washington, DC.
Jan. 17-20, 2006	Ninth round of negotiations held in Washington, DC.
Dec. 16, 2006	Tenth and final round of negotiations concludes in Washington, DC. Chapters on labor and environment left open.
March 30, 2007	President Bush formally notifies Congress of his intention to sign the U.S.-Panama FTA.
April 27, 2007	USTR transmits to the White House and Congress 27 trade advisory reports.
May 10, 2007	Congressional leadership and Bush Administration agree to change language of labor, environment, investment, and intellectual property rights chapters in this and three other proposed FTAs based on principles outlined in a bipartisan agreement.

Date	Milestone
June 28, 2007	The United States and Panama sign a free trade agreement at the Organization of American States in Washington, DC.
July 2, 2007	USTR releases final text of U.S.-Panama FTA.
July 11, 2007	Panama's National Assembly approves U.S.-Panama FTA, 58-4.
November 30, 2010	United States and Panama sign a Tax Information and Exchange Agreement (TIEA).
January 25, 2011	House Ways and Means Committee holds hearing on U.S. free trade agreements with Colombia, Panama, and South Korea.
March 9, 2011	Senate Finance Committee holds hearing on U.S. free trade agreements with Colombia, Panama, and South Korea.
March 30, 2011	House Ways and Means Committee Subcommittee on Trade holds hearing on U.S. free trade agreement with Panama.
April 5, 2011	Panama enacts labor code changes requested by the U.S. Congress and the Obama Administration.
April 18, 2011	Tax Information and Exchange Agreement (TIEA) enters into force in Panama.
May 25, 2011	Senate Finance Committee holds hearing on the Panama FTA.
July 6, 2011	Panama removed from OECD "Gray List" of countries in noncompliance with international tax standard.
July 7, 2011	House Ways and Means and Senate Finance Committees hold "mock markups" on draft implementing bills for U.S.-Panama Free Trade Agreement. House Ways and Means approves 22-2. Senate Finance approves 22-15.
October 3, 2011	President Obama formally submits implementing legislation and required supporting documents to Congress.
October 3, 2011	Identical bills are introduced in the House (H.R. 3079) and the Senate (S. 1643).
October 5, 2011	House Ways and Means Committee orders H.R. 3079 favorably reported by roll call vote, 32-3 (H.Rept. 112-238).
October 6, 2011	House Committee on Rules provides closed rule (H.Res. 425) for consideration of H.R. 3079 under which debate is limited to 90 minutes and all points of order against consideration of H.R. 3079 are waived.
October 11, 2011	Senate Finance Committee orders S. 1643 favorably reported by voice vote, with no written report.
October 12, 2011	H.R. 3079 agreed to in the House, 300-129.
October 12, 2011	H.R. 3079 agreed to in the Senate, 77-22.
October 21, 2011	President Obama signs H.R. 3079 into law (P.L. 112-43, 125 Stat. 427).
October 2012	Panamanian legislature completes work on bills required to bring Panamanian law into compliance with provisions of FTA.
October 22, 2012	The United States and Panama exchange notes providing for the agreement's entry into force on October 31, 2012.

Appendix A. (Continued)

Date	Milestone
October 29, 2012	President Obama implements FTA by presidential proclamation (#8894).
October 31, 2012	U.S.-Panama FTA enters into force.

Source: CRS.

Appendix B. Panama: Selected Economic Indicators

	2001	2002	2003	2004	2005	2006	2007	2008	2009	2010	2011
GDP Growth (%)	0.6	2.2	4.2	7.5	7.2	8.5	12.1	10.1	3.9	7.6	10.6
Per Capita GDP Growth (%)	-1.3	0.4	2.3	5.6	5.3	6.7	10.2	8.3	2.2	5.9	8.9
Unemployment Rate (urban %)	14.0	16.5	15.9	14.1	12.1	10.4	7.8	6.5	7.9	7.7	5.4
Inflation – CPI (%)	0.0	1.8	1.5	1.5	3.4	2.2	6.4	6.8	1.9	4.9	6.1
Current Acct. Bal. (% GDP)	-1.4	-0.8	-4.5	-7.1	-4.9	-3.1	-7.3	-11.5	0.0	-11.4	-12.5
Terms of Trade (2005=100)	na	108.7	103.9	101.9	100.0	97.1	96.2	91.8	96.3	94.4	92.4

Source: United Nations Economic Commission on Latin America and the Caribbean, *Economic Survey of Latin America and the Caribbean,* Summer 2012.

End Notes

[1] For details, see CRS Report RL33743, *Trade Promotion Authority (TPA) and the Role of Congress in Trade Policy*, by J. F. Hornbeck and William H. Cooper.

[2] President Obama also submitted separate implementing bills for the free trade agreements with Colombia and South Korea, as well as legislation that reauthorized trade adjustment assistance. All four bills were considered as part of a trade bargain struck by Congress and the Administration.

[3] Some Members of Congress remain skeptical of provisions in the May 10th agreement. See, U.S. Congress, Senate Committee on Finance, *United States-Panama Trade Promotion Agreement Implementation Act, Report together with Additional Views*, Report to accompany S. 1643, 112th Cong., 2d sess., September 20, 2012, S.Rept. 112-224 (Washington: GPO, 2012), pp. 54-57.

[4] Inside U.S. Trade. *Committee Chairs Signal FTA Problem Over Panama Assembly Head.* September 21, 2007.

[5] U.S. Department of State. Press Statement. *Election of Panamanian National Assembly President Pedro Miguel González-Pinzón.* September 1, 2007.

[6] Len Bracken and Mike Ceaser, "USTR Finishes Prep Work on Panama FTA, Ready for Technical Talks with Lawmakers," *BNA International Trade Reporter*, April 21, 2011, and correspondence with Embassy of Panama, April 8, 2011.

[7] U.S. Department of State. Bureau of Democracy, Human Rights, and Labor. *2010 Country Reports on Human Rights: Panama.* Washington, DC. April 8, 2011.

[8] For more details, see, CRS Report RL30981, *Panama: Political and Economic Conditions and U.S. Relations*, by Mark P. Sullivan and Donald J. Marples.

[9] This standard "requires exchange of information on request in all tax matters for the administration and enforcement of domestic tax law without regard to a domestic tax interest requirement or bank secrecy for tax purposes." *Progress Report on the Jurisdictions Surveyed by the OECD Global Forum in Implementing the International Agreed Tax Standard*, February 18, 2011. The standard has been endorsed by the G20 Finance Ministers and the United Nations Committee of Experts on International Cooperation in Tax Matters.

[10] United States Government Accountability Office (GAO). *International Taxation: Large U.S. Corporations and Federal Contractors with Subsidiaries in Jurisdictions Listed as Tax Havens or Financial Privacy Jurisdictions*. GAO-09-157. December 2008.

[11] So-called "partners of relevance." Inside U.S. Trade. *Administration Signals Panama Issues Not Major FTA Obstacles.* March 13, 2009, and Schatz, Joseph J, "Pending Panama Trade Agreement No Sure Thing as Opponents Mobilize," *CQ Today,* March 11, 2009, p. 6. Panama agreed to implement the OECD tax standard in 2002 through agreements on the exchange of tax information, but delayed entering into any such agreements until 2011.

[12] Organization for Economic Cooperation and Development (OEDC), *Progress Report on the Jurisdictions Surveyed by the OECD Global Forum in Implementing the International Agreed Tax Standard*, July 6, 2011.

[13] Inside U.S. Trade, *Scope, Timing of TAA Renewal Complicates Path Forward for Trade Deals*, April 14, 2011, and International Trade Reporter, *Hatch Challenges Assistance Link to FTAs at Finance Committee Hearing on Panama*, June 2, 2011.

[14] For details, see CRS Report R41922, *Trade Adjustment Assistance (TAA) and Its Role in U.S. Trade Policy*, by J. F. Hornbeck and Laine Elise Rover.

[15] Because TAA legislation on its own would be considered a revenue bill, it could not originate in the Senate. To have the Senate act first on TAA required a legislative vehicle originating in the House that could then be amended in the Senate, in this case, the bill to extend the Generalized System of Preferences.

[16] U.S. Congress, House Committee on Rules, *Providing for Consideration of the Senate Amendment to the Bill (H.R. 2832) to Extend the Generalized System of Preferences and for Other Purposes*, Report to accompany H.Res. 425, 112th Cong., 1st sess., October 6, 2011, H.Rept. 112-240 (Washington: GPO, 2011), pp. 1-3.

[17] Michael L. Conniff, *Panama and the United States: The Forced Alliance*, 2nd ed. (Athens: University of Georgia Press, 2001), pp. 30-35.

[18] Ralph Lee Woodward, *Central America: A Nation Divided*, 3rd ed. (New York: Oxford University Press, 1999), pp. 63-70.

[19] Conniff, *Panama and the United States*, pp. 134-39 and CRS Report RL30981, *Panama: Political and Economic Conditions and U.S. Relations*, by Mark P. Sullivan and Donald J. Marples.

[20] The Economist Intelligence Unit. *Panama: Country Profile 2003.* London, 2003. pp. 16-17; U.S. Department of Energy. Energy Information Administration. *Panama: Country Analysis Briefs*. October 2003; and http://www.pancanal.com.

[21] Ibid.

[22] Government of Panama. *Panama-Pacifico Special Economic Area Agency.*

[23] Ibid., and discussion with IFC official.

[24] Panama's dollarized economy has been a cornerstone of its long-term economic stability. It has safeguarded Panama against exchange rate risk, currency mismatches, and speculative attacks experienced in other developing economies, and eliminated the monetizing of deficits, thereby reinforcing fiscal constraint and price stability. See Juan Luis Moreno-Villalaz, "Financial Integration and Dollarization: The Case of Panama," *Cato Journal*, Winter 2005. For more on trade preferences, see CRS Report RL33951, *U.S. Trade Policy and the Caribbean: From Trade Preferences to Free Trade Agreements*, by J. F. Hornbeck.

[25] United Nations Economic Commission on Latin America and the Caribbean, *Statistical Yearbook for Latin America and the Caribbean 2009* (Washington, DC: United Nations, 2010) and press release December 13, 2010.

[26] Correspondence with Embassy of Panama, December 2010.

[27] Interviews with CFZ representatives, September 21, 2005.

[28] Colón Free Zone User's Association. *Rules of Conduct for the Members of the Colón Free Zone Users' Association*, 1995; and author's interviews with representatives from agencies mentioned.

[29] Services trade data are not available for smaller U.S. trading partners, including Panama.

[30] Technically classified in the Harmonized Tariff System (HTS) as "products of the United States when returned after having been exported, without having been advanced in value or improved in condition by any process."

[31] U.S. Department of Commerce, *Doing Business In Panama: 2008 Country Commercial Guide for U.S. Companies.*

[32] Inside U.S. Trade. *Panama FTA Unlikely To Be Docked Into CAFTA as Talks Set to Begin.* April 23, 2004.

[33] USITC, *U.S.-Panama Trade Promotion Agreement: Potential Economy-wide and Selected Sectoral Effects,* pp. 1-1 and 1-5.

[34] Ibid., pp. 1-5, 2-1, and 2-7.

[35] Ibid., pp. 2-1 and 2-7.

[36] The USITC estimated that 96% of Panamanian exports entered the United States duty free in 2006 under these various preferential arrangements as under normal trade relations (MFN) treatment. Ibid., pp. 1-5.

[37] Office of the United States Trade Representative, *2011 National Trade Estimates Report on Foreign Trade Barriers*, Washington, DC, March 2011, p 281.

[38] Office of the United States Trade Representative. *Free Trade with Panama: Summary of the Agreement.* January 2007.

[39] CRS Report R40622, *Agriculture in Pending U.S. Free Trade Agreements with South Korea, Colombia, and Panama*, by Remy Jurenas.

[40] CRS derived this effective ad valorem equivalent by applying the current U.S. over-quota tariffs against the FY2008 import unit value for such imports. The economic effect is to raise the price of sugar in the United States above the world price, increasing income to sugar-producing industries, but raising costs to sugar-using firms and consumers. See CRS Report R40995, *Sugar Market Developments and Policy Issues*, by Remy Jurenas.

[41] USITC, *U.S.-Panama Trade Promotion Agreement: Potential Economy-wide and Selected Sectoral Effects*, pp. 2-7, 2-10, and 2-18 through 2-19.

[42] Inside U.S. Trade. *Panama FTA Offers Limited Sugar Access; Labor Changes Possible.* December 22, 2006.

[43] United States Trade Representative. *2007 National Trade Estimate Report on Foreign Trade Barriers*. Washington, DC. March 2007. p. 452.

[44] Berrocal, Rafael E. Panamá Reconoce Sistema Sanitario de Estados Unidos. Presna.com. February 22, 2006, and *Inside U.S. Trade*. Dispute Over Agriculture Inspections Holding up U.S.-Panama FTA Talks. January 23, 2006. Also see USTR Press Release, February 13, 2006.

[45] *United States-Panama Agreement Regarding Certain Sanitary and Phytosanitary Measures and Technical Standards Affecting Trade in Agricultural Products*. December 20, 2006.

[46] USTR, *2011 Foreign Trade Barriers*, p. 282.

[47] Inside U.S. Trade. *U.S. Panama FTA Includes Restrictive Textile Rules of Origi*n. January 5, 2007, and USTR, *Free Trade with Panama*, p. 2.

[48] Panamcham. *Issues of Importance in the U.S.-Panama FTA Negotiations*, March 12, 2004. http://www.panamcham.com/business_center/FTA.asp.

[49] USTR, *2011 Foreign Trade Barriers*, pp. 282-283.

[50] Ibid.

[51] Indirect expropriation refers to regulatory and other actions that can adversely affect a business or property owner in a way that is "tantamount to expropriation." This issue and many cases are discussed in CRS Report RL31638, *Foreign Investor Protection Under NAFTA Chapter 11*, by Robert Meltz.

[52] Washington Trade Daily, "Labor's View of US Trade Policy," *Trade Reports International Group*, March 18, 2011.

[53] USITC, *U.S.-Panama Trade Promotion Agreement: Potential Economy-wide and Selected Sectoral Effects*, pp. 3-1.

[54] USTR, *2007 Foreign Trade Barriers*, pp. 455-456.

[55] USTR, *2011 Foreign Trade Barriers*, p. 284.

[56] U.S.-Panama FTA, Chapter 15.

[57] U.S. Congress. House of Representatives. Committee on Ways and Means. *Dominican Republic-Central America-United States Free Trade Agreement Implementation Act*. H.Rept. 109-182. pp. 50-51. The side agreement is available at http://www.ustr.gov and for a summary of the debate, Rosella Brevetti, "CAFTA Opponents Blast U.S. Stance on Guatemalan Data Protection Law," *BNA International Trade Reporter*, March 10, 2005.

[58] There are further complicating implications. This process is useful for countries with weak drug certification mechanisms, but for those that have developed such capability, it may encourage hasty responses or circumventing the process all together to qualify for the six-month time constraint.

[59] The difference is that in most developing countries, the social costs associated with environmental degradation, pollution, and poor working conditions may not be captured in the market price of goods (so-called *external* costs). Through legal and regulatory measures, developed countries require that businesses correct for many of these social costs, thereby *internalizing* them to the business, where they are then reflected in the final (relatively higher) price of the good in the market place.

[60] Dwight H. Perkins, Steven Radelet, and David L. Lindauer, *Economics of Development*, 6th ed. (New York: W. W. Norton Company, 2006), pp. 745-746. Productivity and wage levels are highly correlated, suggesting that lower productivity jobs gravitate toward countries with a relative abundance of low-skilled (and hence low-wage) workers. See also Dani Rodrik, "Sense and Nonsense in the Globalization Debate," *Foreign Policy*, Summer 1997, pp. 30-33.

[61] Some broader evidence suggests that FTAs have not "forced a race to the bottom of regulatory standards," but rather to the contrary, that policy convergence is affected more by countries agreeing to "norms of governance" via cooperation through international agreements. Daniel W. Drezner, "Globalization and Policy Convergence," *International Studies Review*, vol. 3, no. 1 (Spring 2001), pp. 75 and 78.

[62] As defined by the United Nations International Labor Organization (ILO) in the *Fundamental Principles and Rights at Work and its Follow-up (1998) Declaration.*

[63] U.S.-Panama Free Trade Agreement. *Report of the Labor Advisory Committee for Trade Negotiations and Trade Policy (LAC).* April 25, 2007. pp. 3-7, and U.S. Congress. House of Representatives. Committee on Ways and Means. *Dominican Republic-Central America-United States Free Trade Agreement Implementation Act.* H.Rept. 109-182. pp. 47-50.

[64] U.S. Department of State. Bureau of Democracy, Human Rights, and Labor. *2010 Country Reports on Human Rights: Panama.* Washington, DC. April 8, 2011, and American Federation of Labor and Congress of Industrial Organizations (AFL-CIO). *Panama: Labor Rights and Child Labor Reports*. Washington, DC. August 9, 2004. p. 3.

[65] David J Lynch, "U.S.-Panama Trade Deal May Test Obama Goals: Congress Wants to See Bank, Tax Reforms There First," *USA Today*, July 31, 2009, p. B1.

[66] See http://www.sierraclub.org/trade *Principles for Environmentally Responsible Trade.* Another important issue for the United States is ensuring that its higher environmental standards defined in law and regulation not be compromised by challenges of protectionism. See CRS Report RL31638, *Foreign Investor Protection Under NAFTA Chapter 11*, by Robert Meltz.

[67] See Audley, John. *Environment and Trade: The Linchpin to Successful CAFTA Negotiations?* Carnegie Endowment for International Peace. Washington, DC. July 2003.

[68] U.S.-Panama FTA, Chapter 17, The Environment.

[69] Office of the United States Trade Representative. *Interim Environmental Review: U.S.-Panama Free Trade Agreement.* June 2004. pp. 7-9.

[70] Ibid., pp. 15-20.

[71] Government of Panama. Ministry of Trade and Industry. *Panama's National Strategy for Trade Capacity Building (TCB) in Light of the Free Trade Agreement with the United States*. Panama, March 4, 2005. pp. 20-23.

[72] Miller, Eric. *USAID/Panama-Supported TCB Programs.* Summary chapter. Nathan and Associates. May 9, 2007.

In: Progress in Panama
Editor: Charles Bolitno

ISBN: 978-1-62417-932-7

Chapter 3

PANAMA COUNTRY PROFILE*

U.S. Department of State

OFFICIAL NAME: REPUBLIC OF PANAMA

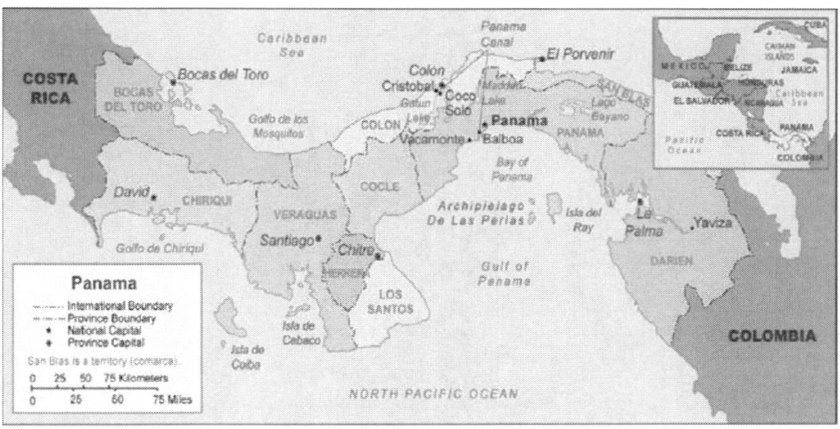

* This is an edited, reformatted and augmented version of U.S. Department of State Publication, dated March 2012.

Flag of Panama.

GEOGRAPHY

Area: 75,517 sq. km. (29,157 sq. mi.); slightly smaller than South Carolina. Panama occupies the southeastern end of the isthmus forming the land bridge between North and South America.

Cities: *Capital*--Panama City (430,299), Panama District (880,691), Panama Province (1,713,000)). *Other cities*--Colon City (34,655), Colon district (206,553), David City (82,907), David District (144,858). Terrain: Mountainous (highest elevation Cerro Volcan Baru, 3,475 m. (11,468 ft.)); coastline 2,857 km. (1,786 mi.).

Climate: Tropical, with average daily rainfall 28 mm. (1 in.) in winter.

PEOPLE

Nationality: *Noun and adjective*--Panamanian(s).

Population (March 2011): 3,405,813. 50.3% of the population lives in Panama province.

Annual population growth rate: 1.84%.

Ethnic groups: Mestizo (mix of African, Indigenous, and European – mostly Spanish – ancestry) 67%, Indigenous 12.3%, African descent 9.2%, Other including Caucasian and Chinese 11.5%.

Religions: Roman Catholic 84%, Protestant 15%, other 1%.

Languages: Spanish (official); various indigenous languages. Many Afro descents from the West Indies speak English and many professional college-educated Panamanians in Panama City are bilingual.

Education: *Years compulsory*—primary grades 1-6, or through age 15. *Attendance*—98.4% for primary school-age children (grades 1-6 or ages 6-11), 73.8% for basic secondary (grades 7-9 or ages 12-14), 44.9% for specialized secondary (grades 10-12 or ages 15-17), 34.9% for tertiary. *Literacy—94.5%* overall; much lower literacy in Comarcas Ngobe Bugle 69.2%, Kuna Yala 71.7%, Embera 77.1%.

Health: *Infant mortality rate* (2009)—12.2 deaths/1,000 live births, higher in Comarcas Embera 32.1%, Kuna Yala 22.3%, and Ngobe Bugle 19.2% and Bocas del Toro 26.6%. *Life expectancy 75.3 77.6* yrs women, 72.8 men (2007).

Work force: 1.532 million: Commerce (wholesale and retail)--17.9%; agriculture, cattle, hunting, silviculture—15.4%; construction—10.6%; industries (manufactures)—8.6%; transportation, storage, postal —6.5% %; private home domestic services—4.6%; public and defense administration—6.2%; hotels and restaurants—5.1%; teaching—5.8%; social and health services—3.7%; financial services—2.0%.

Unemployment (August 2011): 4.5%.

Poverty rate (2011): 28%, extreme poverty 11.4%.

Government Type: Constitutional democracy.

Independence: from Spain, November 28, 1821; separation from Colombia, November 3, 1903.

Constitution: October 11, 1972; amended 1983 and 1994 and reformed in 2004.

Branches: *Executive*--president (chief of state), vice president. (A second vice presidential slot was abolished starting with the 2009 electoral cycle.) *Legislative*--National Assembly (unicameral; 71 members, reduced from 78 to 71 members for May 2009 elections).*Judicial*--Supreme Court.

Subdivisions: Nine provinces and three (indigenous) territories.

Political parties: Panameñista Party (formerly the Arnulfista Party (PA)); Democratic Change (CD); National Liberal Republican Movement (MOLIRENA); Democratic Revolutionary Party (PRD); Popular Party (PP).

Suffrage: Universal at 18.

Economy GDP (2010 est.): $20.86 billion.

Annual growth rate: 10.5% (2011 est.); 7.5% (2010); 3.2% (2009); 10.0% (2008); 12.1% (2007).

Per capita GDP: $5,953 (2010 est.); $5,627 (2009 prelim.); $5,541 (2008); $5,115 (2007); $4,640 (2006).

Natural resources: Timber, copper, gold.

Services (77% of GDP): Finance, insurance, health and medical, transportation, telecommunications, Canal and maritime services, tourism, Colon Free Zone, public administration, and general commerce.

Agriculture, Fishing, Mining (5.7 % of GDP, 2010 est.): *Products*--bananas, corn, sugarcane, rice, coffee, shrimp, timber, vegetables, livestock.

Industry/manufacturing (11.4% of GDP): construction, brewing, cement and other construction materials, sugar milling.

Other: (5.9% of GDP)

Trade (2010): *Exports (goods)*--$725 million in exports, with salmon/tuna as the largest dollar amount, followed by beef, watermelon, shrimp, and pineapples. *Export partners* (as a percentage of total export value in 2010 according to the Government of Panama)--U.S. 29.2%, Canada 10.5%, Netherlands 7.0%, Sweden 6.9%, Costa Rica 6.8%, China (P.R.C.) 5.0%, and Taiwan 5.0%. *Imports (goods)*--$9.1 billion was imported in 2010: petrol and fuel oils, capital goods, foodstuffs, chemicals, and consumer and intermediate goods are the leading imports. *Import partners* (2010 according to the Government of Panama)--the top five countries were the U.S. 27.5%, China 5.4%, Costa Rica 4.9%, Mexico 4.3%, and South Korea 3.2%. *U.S. exports to Panama* (2011 according to the U.S. Census)--$8.25 billion: primarily oil and capital- and technology-intensive manufactured goods. *Panama exports to U.S.* (2011)--$379 million: primarily seafood and repaired goods. Statistics from the Government of Panama and the Government of the United States include only goods which transit the Colon Free Zone into Panama's customs territory.

Foreign direct investment (2010): $2.4 billion.

PEOPLE

Panamanians' culture, customs, and language are predominantly Caribbean Spanish. Because of Panama's unique location as a transit point and because of people coming over the years to work on the railroad and the Canal, the majority of the population is ethnically a mix of Spanish, indigenous, and of African descent. The remaining population is of Afro descent, Caucasian, indigenous, Chinese, and others. Spanish is the official and dominant language; English is a common second language spoken by the West Indians and by many businesspeople and professionals. More than half the population lives in the Panama City-Colon metropolitan corridor.

Panama is rich in folklore and popular traditions. Lively salsa--a mixture of Latin American popular music, rhythm and blues, jazz, and rock--is a Panamanian specialty, and Ruben Blades its best-known performer. Indigenous influences dominate handicrafts such as the famous Kuna textile *molas.* Artist Roberto Lewis' Presidential Palace murals and his restoration work and ceiling in the National Theater are widely admired. Roberto Duran is a famous boxer. Mariano Rivera is a pitcher for the New York Yankees.

As of 2010, more than 117,600 Panamanian students attended the University of Panama, the Technological University, the Autonomous University of Chiriqui, and the University of Santa Maria La Antigua, a private Catholic institution. Including smaller colleges, there are 88 institutions of higher education in Panama. The first 6 years of primary education are compulsory. As of 2010, there were 723,666 students enrolled in primary and secondary school. More than 94.5% of Panamanians are literate.

HISTORY

Panama's history has been shaped by the evolution of the world economy and the ambitions of great powers. The earliest known inhabitants of Panama were the Cuevas and the Coclé tribes, but they were decimated by disease and fighting when the Spanish arrived in the 1500s.

Rodrigo de Bastidas, sailing westward from Venezuela in 1501 in search of gold, was the first European to explore the Isthmus of Panama. A year later, Christopher Columbus visited the Isthmus and established a short-lived settlement in the Darien. Vasco Nunez de Balboa's tortuous trek from the Atlantic to the Pacific in 1513 demonstrated that the Isthmus was, indeed, the path between the seas, and Panama quickly became the crossroads and marketplace of Spain's empire in the New World. Gold and silver were brought by ship from South America, hauled across the Isthmus, and loaded aboard ships for Spain. The route became known as the Camino Real, or Royal Road, although it was more commonly known as *Camino de Cruces* (Road of the Crosses) because of the abundance of gravesites along the way.

Panama was part of the Spanish empire for 300 years (1538-1821). From the outset, Panamanian identity was based on a sense of "geographic destiny," and Panamanian fortunes fluctuated with the geopolitical importance of the Isthmus. The colonial experience also spawned Panamanian nationalism as well as a racially complex and highly stratified society, the source of internal conflicts that ran counter to the unifying force of nationalism.

Building the Canal

Modern Panamanian history has been shaped by its trans-isthmian canal, which had been a dream since the beginning of Spanish colonization. From 1880 to 1890, a French company under Ferdinand de Lesseps attempted unsuccessfully to construct a sea-level canal on the site of the present Panama Canal. In November 1903, with U.S. encouragement, Panama proclaimed its independence and concluded the Hay/Bunau-Varilla Treaty with the United States.

The treaty granted rights to the United States "as if it were sovereign" in a zone roughly 10 miles wide and 50 miles long. In that zone, the U.S. would build a canal, then administer, fortify, and defend it "in perpetuity." In 1914, the United States completed the existing 83-kilometer (52 mile) canal, which is one of the world's greatest feats of engineering. The early 1960s saw the beginning of sustained pressure in Panama for the renegotiation of this treaty.

Military Coups and Coalitions

From 1903 until 1968, Panama was a constitutional democracy dominated by a commercially oriented oligarchy. During the 1950s, the Panamanian military began to challenge the oligarchy's political hegemony. In October 1968, Dr. Arnulfo Arias Madrid, twice elected president and twice ousted by the Panamanian military, was ousted for a third time as president by the National Guard after only 10 days in office. A military government was established, and the commander of the National Guard, Brigadier General Omar Torrijos, soon emerged as the principal power in Panamanian political life. Torrijos' regime was harsh and corrupt, but his charisma, populist domestic programs, and nationalist (anti-U.S.) foreign policy appealed to the rural and urban constituencies largely ignored by the oligarchy.

Torrijos' death in 1981 altered the tone but not the direction of Panama's political evolution. Despite the 1983 constitutional amendments, which appeared to proscribe a political role for the military, the Panama Defense Forces (PDF), as they were then known, continued to dominate Panamanian political life behind a facade of civilian government. By this time, General Manuel Noriega was firmly in control of both the PDF and the civilian government.

The United States froze economic and military assistance to Panama in the summer of 1987 in response to the domestic political crisis in Panama and an attack on the U.S. Embassy. In April 1988, President Reagan invoked the International Emergency Economic Powers Act, freezing Panamanian Government assets in all U.S. organizations. In May 1989 Panamanians voted overwhelmingly for the anti-Noriega candidates. The Noriega regime promptly annulled the election, and embarked on a new round of repression.

By the fall of 1989 the regime was barely clinging to power, and the regime's paranoia made daily existence unsafe for American citizens.

On December 20, 1989, President George H.W. Bush ordered the U.S. military into Panama to protect U.S. lives and property, to fulfill U.S. treaty responsibilities to operate and defend the Canal, to assist the Panamanian people in restoring democracy, and to bring Noriega to justice. The U.S. troops involved in Operation Just Cause achieved their primary objectives quickly, and Noriega eventually surrendered to U.S. authorities. He completed his sentence for drug trafficking charges in September 2007. In August 2007, a U.S. federal court in Miami found Noriega extraditable to France to serve a sentence imposed there after an *in absentia* conviction for money laundering. Noriega was extradited to France in April 2010 after exhausting all his appeals in U.S. courts, and was sentenced to a 7-year prison term. In December 2011, French authorities returned Noriega to Panama, where he remains in prison facing charges of aggravated murder.

Rebuilding Democracy

Panama's Electoral Tribunal moved quickly to rebuild the civilian constitutional government, reinstated the results of the May 1989 election on December 27, 1989, and confirmed the victory of President Guillermo Endara and Vice Presidents Guillermo Ford and Ricardo Arias Calderon.

During its 5-year term, the often-fractious Endara government struggled to meet the public's high expectations. Its new police force was a major improvement over its predecessor but was not fully able to deter crime. Ernesto Perez Balladares was sworn in as President on September 1, 1994, after an internationally monitored election campaign.

Perez Balladares ran as the candidate for a three-party coalition dominated by the Democratic Revolutionary Party (PRD), the erstwhile political arm of military dictatorships. Perez Balladares worked skillfully during the campaign to rehabilitate the PRD's image, emphasizing the party's populist Torrijos roots rather than its association with Noriega. He won the election with only 33% of the vote when the major non-PRD forces splintered into competing factions. His administration carried out economic reforms and often worked closely with the U.S. on implementation of the Canal treaties.

On September 1, 1999, Mireya Moscoso, the widow of former President Arnulfo Arias Madrid, took office after defeating PRD candidate Martin Torrijos, son of the late dictator, in a free and fair election. During her administration, Moscoso attempted to strengthen social programs, especially for child and youth development, protection, and general welfare. Moscoso's administration successfully handled the Panama Canal transfer and was effective in the administration of the Canal.

The PRD's Martin Torrijos won the presidency and a legislative majority in the National Assembly in 2004. Under Torrijos, Panama continued strong economic growth and initiated the Panama Canal expansion project.

In May 2009, Panama held general elections and selected Ricardo Martinelli as president. President Martinelli assumed the presidency on July 1, 2009 and promised to promote free trade, establish a Panama City metro system, reform the health care system, and complete the expansion plan for the Panama Canal.

GOVERNMENT AND POLITICAL CONDITIONS

Panama is a representative democracy with three branches of government: executive and legislative branches elected by direct vote for 5-year terms, and an appointed judiciary. The judicial branch is organized under a nine-member Supreme Court (each judge is appointed for a 10-year term) and includes all tribunals and municipal courts. An autonomous Electoral Tribunal supervises voter registration, the election process, and the activities of political parties. Anyone over the age of 18 may vote.

Principal Government Officials

President--Ricardo MARTINELLI
Vice President--Juan Carlos VARELA
Minister of Foreign Affairs--Roberto HENRIQUEZ
Ambassador to the United States--Mario E. JARAMILLO
Ambassador to the Organization of American States--Guillermo COCHEZ

Panama maintains an embassy in the United States at 2862 McGill Terrace, NW, Washington, DC 20008 (tel: 202-483-1407), and consulates in Washington DC, Honolulu, Houston, Miami, New Orleans, New York, Philadelphia, San Juan, San Diego, and Tampa.

National Security

Following a restructuring in July 2010, the Panamanian Security Forces consist of the Panamanian National Police (PNP), the National Frontier Service (Servicio Nacional de Fronteras or SENAFRONT), the National Aero-Naval Service (Servicio Nacional Aero-Naval or SENAN), and the Institutional Protection Service (SPI--a secret service equivalent). A constitutional amendment passed in 1994 permanently abolished the military.

The lead criminal investigative entity is the Judicial Investigative Directorate (DIJ), which was previously under the nominal direction of the autonomous Attorney General and known as the Technical Judicial Police (PTJ). The DIJ is now part of the PNP, though it maintains investigative links with the Attorney General's office.

Economy

Panama's economy is based primarily on a well-developed services sector that accounts for about 77% of GDP. Services include the Panama Canal, banking, the Colon Free Zone, insurance, container ports, flagship registry, tourism, and medical and healthcare.

In October 2006, Panamanians voted overwhelmingly in favor of a $5.25 billion Canal expansion project to construct a third set of locks, which is expected to be completed in 2014.

The Government of Panama expects the project to help maintain the value of this strategic transportation asset by doubling the capacity of the waterway. The expansion is financed through a combination of loans from multilateral institutions and current revenues.

GDP growth in 2011 surpassed 10%. Recent growth has been fueled by government investment in infrastructure as well as the construction, transportation, maritime, tourism sectors, and Panama Canal-related activities. Panama maintains one of the most positive growth rates in the region. As a result of this growth and sound fiscal management, government debt as a percentage of GDP dropped to 41.2% in 2011, and government-issued debt is classified as the lowest rung of investment grade.

Socially, poverty has fallen from 32.7% in 2008 to about 28% in 2011, with a reduction in the extreme poverty rate from 18.8% in 1997 to 11.4% in

2011. The distribution of income, while improving slightly in recent years, remains among the most unequal in the hemisphere.

Panama has bilateral free trade agreements (FTAs) in force with Peru, Chile, El Salvador, Taiwan, Singapore, Guatemala, Honduras, Nicaragua, and Costa Rica, and has completed negotiations with Canada and the European Union. Panama has started free trade negotiations with Colombia, and EFTA. The U.S. and Panama signed a Trade Promotion Agreement (TPA) in June 2007.

The agreement was overwhelmingly approved in July 2007 by the Panamanian National Assembly. In April 2011, Panama completed indicated steps relating to labor code and tax transparency to ready the Trade Agreement for submission to the United States Congress. The Trade Agreement was passed by the U.S. Congress and signed by President Obama in October 2011, and both countries are working to bring the agreement into force. Once implemented, the agreement will promote economic opportunity by eliminating tariffs and other barriers to trade of goods and services and will provide a framework for any trade disputes.

Foreign Relations

Panama is a member of the UN General Assembly and most major UN agencies. It maintains membership in several international financial institutions, including the World Bank, the Inter-American Development Bank, and the International Monetary Fund.

Panama is a member of the Organization of American States, was a founding member of the Rio Group, and participates in the Community of Latin American and Caribbean States (CELAC). An important aspect of Panama's foreign policy is to maintain the neutrality of the Panama Canal.

Panama is a member of the Central American Integration System (SICA). In 2009 Panama began the process of withdrawing from the Central American Parliament (Parlacen), but in January 2012, the Supreme Court overturned the law that had originally withdrawn its participation.

Panama joined its six Central American neighbors at the 1994 Summit of the Americas in signing the Alliance for Sustainable Development, known as the Conjunta Centroamerica-USA or CONCAUSA, to promote sustainable economic development in the region.

U.S.-Panamanian Relations

The United States cooperates with the Panamanian Government in promoting economic, democratic, security, and social development through U.S. and international agencies. Cultural ties between the two countries are strong, and many Panamanians come to the United States for higher education and advanced training. In 2007, the U.S. and Panama partnered to launch a regional health worker training center. The center provides training to community healthcare workers in Panama and throughout Central America. At any given time, there are approximately 45,000 American citizens in Panama, including tourists and those who reside in Panama, such as retirees from the Panama Canal Commission and individuals who hold dual nationality. There is a rapidly growing enclave of American retirees in the Chiriqui Province in western Panama.

In the economic investment arena, the Panamanian Government has been successful in the enforcement of intellectual property rights. Panama has concluded a Bilateral Investment Treaty Amendment with the United States and an agreement with the Overseas Private Investment Corporation. Although money laundering remains a problem, Panama passed significant reforms in 2000 intended to strengthen its cooperation against international financial crimes.

The Panama Canal Treaties

The 1977 Panama Canal Treaties entered into force on October 1, 1979. They replaced the 1903 Hay/Bunau-Varilla Treaty between the United States and Panama (modified in 1936 and 1955), and all other U.S.-Panama agreements concerning the Panama Canal, which were in force on that date. The treaties comprise a basic treaty governing the operation and defense of the Canal from October 1, 1979 to December 31, 1999 (Panama Canal Treaty) and a treaty guaranteeing the permanent neutrality of the Canal (Neutrality Treaty).

The details of the arrangements for U.S. operation and defense of the Canal under the Panama Canal Treaty are spelled out in separate implementing agreements. The Canal Zone and its government ceased to exist when the treaties entered into force and Panama assumed jurisdiction over Canal Zone territories and functions, a process that was finalized on December 31, 1999.

INDEX

D

E

H

I

N

O

P

T

U

V

W

Y